SECOND EDI

IN CHARGE 1

An Integrated Skills Course for High-Level Students

Evelina Dimitrova-Galaczi
Árpád Galaczi

Consulting authors
James E. Purpura
Diane Pinkley

LONGMAN ON THE **WEB**

Longman.com offers online resources for teachers and students. Access our Companion Websites, our online catalog, and our local offices around the world.

Longman English Success offers online courses to give learners flexible study options. Courses cover General English, Business English, and Exam Preparation.

Visit us at **longman.com** and **englishsuccess.com**.

Longman

In Charge 1, Second Edition

Pearson Education, 10 Bank Street, White Plains, NY 10606

Vice president, director of publishing: Allen Ascher
Editorial manager: Pam Fishman
Project manager: Margaret Grant
Senior development editor: Eleanor Barnes
Vice president, director of design and production: Rhea Banker
Executive managing editor: Linda Moser
Production manager: Liza Pleva
Production coordinator: Melissa Leyva
Production editor/Reprint manager: Robert Ruvo
Director of manufacturing: Patrice Fraccio
Senior manufacturing buyer: Edie Pullman
Photo research: Jennifer McAliney
Cover design: Tracey Cataldo
Text composition: Design 5 Creatives
Text font: 11/14 Palatino
Illustrations: Susan Dietrich, pp. 24, 33, 85, 109, 125; Tim Haggerty, pp. 5, 48,
  153; Greg Harris, p. 4; Chris Reed, pp. 7, 28; Phil Scheuer, pp. 45, 57, 71, 95,
  137, 140, 149; Steve Sullivan, pp. 107, 111, 132, 154
Text credits and photo credits: see p. viii

Library of Congress Cataloging-in-Publication Data

Dimitrova-Galaczi, Evelina, 1967–
    In charge 1 : an integrated skills course for high-level students / Evelina
Dimitrova-Galaczi, Árpád Galaczi ; consulting authors James E. Purpura,
Diane Pinkley.—2nd ed.
      p. cm.
    ISBN 0-13-094264-2
      1. English language—Textbooks for foreign speakers. I. Galaczi, Árpád, 1971–

PE1128 .D475 2002
428.2'4—dc21

                                          2002025279

Printed in the United States of America
1 2 3 4 5 6 7 8 9 10-WC-06 05 04 03 02

CONTENTS

SCOPE AND SEQUENCE

UNIT	Functions	Grammar	Listen	Pronunciation
■ 1 ■ **Food for Thought** Page 3	• Giving personal information • Stating preferences • Describing habits • Suggesting remedies	**Review of present tenses:** • simple present • present progressive • present perfect • present perfect progressive • stative verbs	A pizza maker gives a talk on the origins of pizza ➡ Listening for gist and details	–*s* endings in present tense verbs and plural nouns
■ 2 ■ **Memorable Moments** Page 15	• Giving information about past events • Asking for more information • Describing experiences	**Review of past tenses:** • simple past • past progressive • past perfect	A conversation about personal firsts ➡ Listening for sequence	Verbs and adjectives
■ 3 ■ **The Future of Film** Page 27	• Asking for and making predictions • Giving opinions • Offering evidence for opinions • Reaching a compromise	**Review of future:** • *will* • *going to* • simple present • present progressive	A panel discussion on digital technology's effects on films ➡ Evaluating arguments	Differing stress patterns for noun/verb homophones
PROGRESS CHECK (Units 1–3) ■ Page 39				
■ 4 ■ **I Beg to Differ** Page 43	• Describing a conflict • Empathizing • Asking for and giving advice • Disagreeing politely	**Gerunds and infinitives:** • subject position • object position • changes in meaning • *It's* adjective + infinitive	A lecture on conflict resolution ➡ Applying background knowledge	Using contrastive stress
■ 5 ■ **Odd Jobs** Page 55	• Describing jobs • Stating abilities • Conveying likes and dislikes • Expressing surprise	**Passive voice:** • simple present • present progressive • simple past • past progressive • past perfect	A radio interview with a storm chaser ➡ Recognizing categories	Using stress and rhythm patterns in compound nouns and adjectives
■ 6 ■ **Beholding Beauty** Page 67	• Describing traits • Specifying details • Talking about regrets • Speculating about the future	**Conditionals:** • first • second • third	A lecture on the role of symmetry in beauty ➡ Identifying cause and effect relationships	Using intonation for stress
PROGRESS CHECK (Units 4–6) ■ Page 79				

Speak Out	Read About It	Write About It	Discussion Topics
Stages of discussions ➡ Opening a meeting or discussion	"Coffee: The World's Most Popular Beverage" ➡ Using contextual clues	Reviewing audience and purpose ➡ Linking paragraphs to essays	• The social role of food • Influences behind food preferences • Traditional remedies
Defining social issues: ➡ Defining an issue	"Paul McCready's Flying Circus" ➡ Perceiving time organization	Responding to an essay question ➡ Analyzing essay questions	• Significant personal events • Important moments in history • Risk-taking
Debating the ethics of producing violent films ➡ Speaking persuasively	"Technology and the Future of Film" ➡ Reading critically	Writing a persuasive essay ➡ Analyzing a persuasive essay	• New technologies and the film industry • Virtual reality • Virtual actors
Resolving a conflict ➡ Managing conflict	"Say What You Mean: Communication Breakdowns" ➡ Evaluating point of view	Writing a composition on conflict ➡ Choosing and narrowing a topic	• Personal conflicts • Conflict management styles • Communication styles • Intercultural communication styles
Explaining and paraphrasing ➡ Maintaining understanding	"A Sweet Job: Ice-cream Taster" ➡ Using graphic organizers	Writing an introductory paragraph of an essay ➡ Analyzing introductions	• Unusual jobs • Dream jobs • Advantages and disadvantages of different careers
Giving opinions on fashion fads ➡ Keeping a discussion on track	"Our Obsession with Beauty: a History" ➡ Evaluating supporting examples	Writing good supporting paragraphs ➡ Analyzing supporting paragraphs	• Differing standards of beauty • Yearly budget spent on appearance • The social advantages of attractiveness

SCOPE AND SEQUENCE

UNIT	Functions	Grammar	Listen	Pronunciation
■ 7 ■ **Feeling Left Out** Page 83	• Describing problems • Describing objects • Offering solutions • Giving additional information	**Relative clauses:** • identifying • non-identifying	A lecture on the brain ➡ Listening to summarize	Linking and assimilation
■ 8 ■ **You're Not My Type** Page 95	• Describing personality traits • Explaining preferences • Requesting specifics	**Phrasal verbs:** • separable • non-separable	A conversation about birth order ➡ Personalizing information	Stressed syllables in phrasal verbs
■ 9 ■ **Tech Trends** Page 107	• Describing changes • Speculating about future trends • Evaluating behavior • Stating needs	**Definite and indefinite articles:** • reference • countability	A conversation about tech pets ➡ Identifying implications	Using stress to confirm information

PROGRESS CHECK (Units 7–9) ■ Page 119

UNIT	Functions	Grammar	Listen	Pronunciation
■ 10 ■ **Space Exploration** Page 123	• Stating and defending opinions • Making predictions • Discussing probability	**Future forms:** • future progressive • future perfect	A class discussion about Planet X ➡ Interpreting relationships between ideas	Emphasizing new information
■ 11 ■ **Adventure Travel** Page 135	• Comparing and contrasting • Describing experiences • Expressing regret • Making complaints	**Wishes and regrets:** • *I wish…* • *Had I known…* • *If only…*	Three radio commentaries ➡ Identifying tone	Forming thought groups
■ 12 ■ **A Way with Words** Page 147	• Reporting information • Giving interpretations • Paraphrasing • Agreeing and disagreeing	**Reported speech:** • reported statements • reported questions • reporting verbs	A panel discussion on Esperanto ➡ Drawing conclusions	Expressing emotion with intonation

PROGRESS CHECK (Units 10–12) ■ Page 159

Speak Out	Read About It	Write About It	Discussion Topics
Planning an awareness campaign ➡ Keeping a discussion going	"Life in the Left Lane" ➡ Evaluating generalizations	Writing a conclusion ➡ Analyzing concluding paragraphs	• Difficulties faced by left-handers • Brain activity and handedness
Planning a class project ➡ Having the floor	"Personality's Part and Parcel" ➡ Making inferences	Analyzing compare and contrast essays ➡ Organizing information	• Blood type and personal traits • Birth order and character • Factors that influence personality
Discussing trends in technology ➡ Managing disruptive behavior	"Enhanced Intelligence: A Smart Idea?": Genetic Engineering ➡ Assessing purpose and function	Writing a point by point essay of comparison ➡ Using transition expressions for comparison	• Computer ethics • Computer fraud • Tech pets • Genetic engineering

Speak Out	Read About It	Write About It	Discussion Topics
Debating use of funds ➡ Citing sources for support	"A Hotel with a Million Stars" ➡ Applying concepts to new information	Block-style essay of comparison ➡ Analyzing block-style organization	• Probability of space tourism • Role of exploration in developing new technology • Exploring new frontiers
Planning an excursion ➡ Endorsing others' opinions	"Junko Tabei: Conqueror of Mountains" ➡ Recognizing comparisons and contrasts	Writing block style essay of contrast ➡ Using transition expressions for contrast	• Dream vacations • Risk and excitement • Situations we wish had gone differently
Concluding a discussion on translation ➡ Closing a discussion	Two translations of Rilke's "The Panther" ➡ Focusing on language choice and style	Self- and peer editing ➡ Using a checklist for self-assessment in writing	• Comic mistranslations • Favorite quotes • Role of translators • Pros and cons of a global language

ACKNOWLEDGMENTS

To our families, Maria, Árpád and Juli, Kate, Simeon and Dessy. And most of all, to our little masterpiece, Danika.

Writing a textbook is full of highs and lows, frustrations, and joys. It would have been impossible to make it to the end without the support of all the people who were, directly or indirectly, involved in this endeavor. This book is as much theirs as ours. To all those people we extend our thanks. Our gratitude goes to Jim Purpura, for having confidence in us and involving us in this project, to Diane Pinkley, for her unflagging dedication to this project, to Deborah Gordon for sharing her talent and her patience with us, and to Eleanor Barnes for her editorial expertise, professionalism, and sense of humor at times when we needed it most. We also wish to thank Marilyn Hochman, for getting us started in the first stage of the journey, and Liz Iannotti and Sylvia Bloch, for being always ready to do last-minute research. Last, but not least, our thanks go to our friends, who have always been a tremendous source of support, inspiration, and encouragement for us. Thank you.

The authors and editors also wish to thank the teachers and students who contributed to this edition through interviews, reviews, and piloting reports. In particular, we wish to acknowledge:

Michelle Merritt-Ascencio: Universidad de Guadalajara, Dept. de Lenguas Modernas Proulex, Gualdajara, Mexico

Stephen Gudgel, Institute of North American Studies, Barcelona, Spain

Duk Rak Joo: Lincoln High School, Tacoma, WA

Terry Hirsch: Waukegan High School, Foreign Language Dept, Waukegan, IL

Photo credits: p. 1, ©Image 100/Royalty-Free/CORBIS; p. 3, (l) ©Bob Krist/CORBIS; p. 3 (r) ©Claudia Kunin/CORBIS; p. 10, © Najlah Feanny/CORBIS; p. 11, © Catherine Karnow/CORBIS; p. 12, © Kennan Ward/CORBIS; p. 14, Reprinted with permission from Greg Tuft, © 2000; p. 15, (c) NASA/Goddard Space Flight Center; p. 15, (r) © Hulton-Deutsch Collection/CORBIS; p. 16, (t) © Bettmann/CORBIS; p. 16, (b) ©AFP/CORBIS; p. 17, ©Bettmann/CORBIS; p. 20, ©Reuters NewMedia Inc./CORBIS; p. 27, ©Adam Woolfitt/CORBIS; p. 36, ©AFP/CORBIS; p. 43, ©Bettmann/CORBIS; p. 49, ©D. Boone/CORBIS; p. 50, ©Image 100/Royalty-Free/CORBIS; p. 55, ©Bettmann/CORBIS; p. 56, ©Ronnen Eshel/CORBIS; p. 59, MondoNovo Maschere, by Guerrino Lovato, Dorsoduro 3063, Venice; p. 60, ©Jim Zuckerman/CORBIS; p. 64, ©Richard T. Nowitz/CORBIS; p. 66, (l) ©AFP/CORBIS; p. 66, (c) ©Gregor Schmid/CORBIS; p. 66, (r) ©Peter Johnson/CORBIS; p. 67, (l) ©Tiziana and Gianni Baldizzone/CORBIS; p. 67, (r) Mitchell Gerber/CORBIS; p. 73, ©Paul Almasy/CORBIS; p. 83, (l) ©CinemaPhoto/CORBIS; p. 83, (c) ©Austrian Archives/CORBIS; p. 83, (r) ©AP/Wide World Photos; p. 91, ©Bettmann/CORBIS; p. 92, ©Mitchell Gerber/CORBIS; p. 112, ©AFP/CORBIS; p. 123, ©Bettmann/CORBIS; p. 128, ©Roger Ressmeyer/CORBIS; p. 129, ©Roger Ressmeyer/CORBIS; p. 135, ©Lowell Georgia/CORBIS; p. 144, © AP/Wide World Photos; p. 147, ©AFP/CORBIS; p. 157, ©Tom Brakefield/CORBIS

Text credits: p. 17, From LITERARY CAVALCADE, January 1997 issue. Copyright ©1997 by Scholastic Inc. Reprinted by permission of Scholastic Inc.; p. 24-25, Reprinted with permission from Mark Wheeler, ©1999; p. 52-53, Paulette Dale and James C. Wolf, ©2000 Addison Wesley Longman; p. 157, (l) From Rainer Maria Rilke, SELECTED POEMS. BILINGUAL EDITION. Edited/translated by C.F. MacIntyre. ©1940 1968 C.F. MacIntyre. Reprinted with permission from University of California Press; p. 157, (r) From THE SELECTED POETRY OF RAINER MARIA RILKE by Rainer Maria Rilke, translated by Stephen Mitchell, copyright ©1982 by Stephen Mitchell. Used by permission of Random House, Inc.

When you learn another language, you also learn about the people who use that language. In this class, you will have opportunities to learn about the customs, concerns, and goals of people from other cultures. You will also have opportunities to share your own thoughts and experiences with your classmates and teacher. Begin by introducing yourself and giving one reason you are studying English.

Getting Acquainted

When you get acquainted with people, you find out information about them. This can sometimes take a long time.

 Get acquainted with your classmates by asking questions using the cues. Write the name of each person who fits each description in the chart. Try to find a different person for each item.

Find someone who...	Person's Name
1. likes to ski	
2. is a vegetarian	
3. likes horror movies	
4. plays a stringed instrument	
5. doesn't like sweets	
6. plays tennis well	
7. loves to sing	
8. likes to travel	
9. knows Greek	
10. Your own idea	
11. Your own idea	
12. Your own idea	

2 Choose two names from your chart and get better acquainted with them. Find out at least five interesting things about each one.

3 Setting realistic goals is an important step in achieving success. You can use your strengths and weaknesses to help you achieve your goals. Think about your goals for this class and complete the chart with your ideas.

Skill	Strengths	Weaknesses	Goal
Grammar			
Listening			
Speaking			
Pronunciation			
Reading			
Writing			

4 Work in small groups. Compare your completed charts and discuss your goals. Are the goals realistic? Are they easily measured? Offer each other advice on ways to accomplish your goals.

5 Work in groups of three. Take turns orally completing the sentences below. The first person can begin with any word. The next person has to fill in the blanks with words that start the last sound in the previous sentence.

    a. I'm going to ____(China)____.

    b. I'm taking a(n) __(accordion)__, three ____(ants)____, and one ____(apple)____.

    c. I'll eat ____(lettuce)____ and drink __(lemonade)__.

    d. I'll buy eight __(diamonds)__ and one ____(dog)____.

    e. Your own idea

    f. Your own idea

FOOD FOR THOUGHT

Unit 1

GETTING STARTED

Warm Up

In addition to sustaining life, food plays a very important role in our social lives. People around the world eat special foods on holidays and at traditional family celebrations. They eat other foods because they're in the mood for them.

1 What foods do you eat on special occasions? Work with a partner and compare your answers.

2 Which factors generally influence your food choices? Rank them from the most important (1) to the least important (6). Compare your rankings with your partner's.

_____ convenience _____ nutrition _____ calories
_____ taste _____ family tradition _____ other

3 Listen to a conversation among three friends and note the snack foods they mention. Share your information with the class.

Figure It Out

 A Korean proverb says that "Eating is heaven." Why we choose to eat the foods we do is the result of many different factors, only one of which is enjoyment. Read the article to find out what they are.

Why We Eat What We Eat
by Karen Odom

Candied grasshoppers are considered mouthwatering treats in China and parts of West Africa, just as roasted caterpillars are prized dishes in parts of south Africa. Many French and Argentinians delight in dinners of

10 horse meat, while Scots eat haggis, a dish made with sheep's stomach. North Americans and Europeans savor fermented cheeses, while many Mexicans happily consume *huitlacoche*,
15 a fungus that grows on corn.

What makes us choose the foods we do, and what makes certain foods desirable in one country but not in another? When we are selecting,
20 preparing, and consuming food, what motivates us to choose certain foods over others is a complex blend of several factors—the food we ate during our childhoods, the geography and climate
25 of our countries, the associations we make with specific foods and holidays, our countries' national customs and traditions, and our personal preferences.

Consuming foods for pleasure can
30 be traced back to our experiences as infants when we associated food with comfort, human contact, and enjoyment. Later as adults, without even realizing it, we reach for the same foods that
35 comforted us in the past. For example, chicken soup was served when we were sick; ice cream or chocolate cake was served on special occasions.

The foods we have grown up with
40 also depend on geography and climate. Since Japan is surrounded by water, it is not surprising that the Japanese diet is rich in fish and seaweed. Countries in tropical zones, such as Brazil, cultivate
45 many grains and fruits that have not been easily recognized in other countries until recently. People from northern countries with plentiful forests are accustomed to eating game, such as rabbit, deer, and
50 pheasant.

Folklore and myth play important roles in the selection of the foods we eat as well, especially for holidays and celebrations. In Greece, for instance, a
55 cake containing a single silver coin is served on New Year's Day. Whoever finds the coin is said to have good luck throughout the coming year. In Italy on New Year's, people eat lentils, which are
60 thought to resemble money. In many countries around the world, cakes of different kinds are served on birthdays, often with candles and decorative designs.

65 As we travel from country to country, we are becoming more familiar with other customs, food preferences, and traditions. Consequently, our food choices will continue to grow in range
70 and sophistication. Before long, it may be just as common to eat tripe in the U.S. as it is in France or Italy, or to enjoy tamales in Korea. The world may at last be united over the dinner table.

5 **Vocabulary Check** Match the expressions on the left with their meanings on the right.

_____ **1.** mouthwatering (line 2)   **a.** combination, mixture
_____ **2.** delight in (line 9)   **b.** found to result from
_____ **3.** blend (line 22)   **c.** delicious, appetizing
_____ **4.** traced back to (line 30)   **d.** to look like, to be similar
_____ **5.** resemble (line 60)   **e.** to make understood
_____ **6.** range (line 69)   **f.** enjoy, appreciate
    g. variety, number of choices

6 What are some foods that bring back childhood memories for you? What foods from other cultures do you like and dislike? In what circumstances did you taste these foods for the first time? Share your experiences with your partner.

Talk About It

7 A researcher and a subject are discussing traditional health foods. Work with a partner. Take turns being the researcher and the subject and discuss the remedies below. Use the conversation as a model.

Example: gargle salty water for a sore throat/use cough drops

ROLES	MODEL CONVERSATION	FUNCTIONS
Researcher:	Have you ever gargled with salty water for a sore throat?	Ask about a remedy.
Subject:	Not really.	Answer the question.
Researcher:	So what do you usually do for a sore throat?	Ask a follow-up question.
Subject:	I usually just ignore it until I feel really bad. But right now I'm using cough drops because I have a sore throat and a cough.	Answer the question and elaborate.

<u>Remedies</u>
a. drink chamomile tea for insomnia/meditate
b. eat chicken soup for flu/take vitamin C
c. drink coffee to stay alert/drink Coke or Pepsi
d. eat papaya for indigestion/drink ginger-ale
e. eat avocados for dry skin/use cream
f. (your own idea)

The Simple Present and Present Progressive Tenses

These examples show how the simple present tense is used.

> 1. Many people **drink** a glass of orange juice in the morning.
>
> 2. **Do** you ever **eat** chocolate when you are upset?
>
> 3. People **consume** food in order to live.
>
> 4. Vegetarians **eliminate** meat from their diet.
>
> 5. The Chinese cooking class **starts** at 11:00 A.M.
>
> 6. I **am** seldom confused about cooking, but I **don't** really **understand** this recipe.

These examples show how the present progressive tense is used.

> 7. The bread **is baking** now.
>
> 8. The vegetables **are** still **boiling**.
>
> 9. I'm getting a new microwave oven tomorrow.
>
> 10. Carolyn **isn't following** her diet anymore.

 1 **Check Your Understanding** Match the example sentences from the boxes with their rules below.

   _9_   **a.** We can use the present progressive to talk about planned actions in the future.

   _____   **b.** We can use the simple present to talk about actions or states in the future.

   _____   **c.** We use the simple present to talk about states, habitual actions, facts, and things that are generally considered to be true.

   _____   **d.** We use the simple present with adverbs of frequency to talk about how often states and actions occur.

   _____   **e.** We use the present progressive in negative sentences with *anymore* to talk about an action that has stopped.

   _____   **f.** We use the present progressive to talk about actions in progress at the present moment.

   _____   **g.** We use the present progressive to talk about actions in progress at the present moment that might continue into the future.

Stative Verbs

Stative verbs refer to states or conditions rather than to actions. They are generally not used in the progressive form. They usually appear in the simple form even though they might describe states which are in progress at the present moment.

Verbs that express . . .	
being and possession	Pretzels **are** my favorite snack.
	Janine **has** over 200 cookbooks in her collection.
intellectual states	**Do** you **believe** that vitamin C prevents colds?
emotions/attitudes	Vince **hates** anything made with mayonnaise.
perceptions/senses	**Can** you **smell** that delicious stew?
wants/needs	**Don't** you **want** the rest of your dessert?

In special cases, stative verbs can appear in the progressive. For example, emphasizing the beginning or the slow progress of an action. (*I'm understanding now.* = *I'm beginning to understand.*) *Be* and *have* are used in the progressive form when they carry a special meaning other than existence (*be*) or possession (*have*).

I **have** two sons, and now they **are having** a fight over the last cookie. (They're fighting.)

The chef **is** usually a pleasant guy, but today he **is being** rude. (He is acting rude.)

2 A commentator for the TV program *Super Chefs* is describing a cooking contest between two competing master chefs. Complete the passage with the appropriate form of the verb in parentheses.

Right now, I **(1. observe)** _am observing_ Master Chef Steve Albanese as he assembles the items for his seafood presentation. It **(2. look)** _____ like he **(3. build)** _____ a delicate tower of ingredients, among them lobster, the theme of today's competition. Chef Albanese usually **(4. prefer)** _____ Italian dishes and traditional, less trendy presentations. Today, however, I **(5. see)** _____ a new, designer-style quality to his food. Oops! He almost lost the shrimp, which he **(6. attempt)** _____ to stack on top of the lobster base. He's OK now, and he **(7. use)** _____ seaweed to help stabilize his tower. A specialty of his is pasta fagioli, a bean soup, which is so wonderful it **(8. bring)** _____ tears to my eyes when I **(9. think)** _____ of it. Now let's check on how Chef Yu, **(10. do)** _____ . Well, viewers, Chef Yu **(11. appear)** _____ to be almost finished. He **(12. pour)** _____ each of three sauces into bowls. I **(13. believe)** _____ he **(14. plan)** _____ to use them to complement the delicate flavor of the lobster his assistants **(15. grill)** _____ . What a contest today!

The Present Perfect and the Present Perfect Progressive Tenses

The present perfect tense (*have/has* + past participle of the verb), relates an action in the past continuing up to the present. Sometimes the present perfect is accompanied by signal words (*already, yet, since*). These need not appear for the meaning of the sentence to be clear.

> **1.** Who **has eaten** all of my tortilla chips?
>
> **2.** He **has worked** as a pastry chef for five years.
>
> **3.** I**'ve** just **tasted** the spaghetti sauce, and it's perfect!
>
> **4. Have** they ever **tried** Thai food before?
>
> **5.** I**'ve been** here since 7:30 P.M. I'm starving!
>
> **6.** Margo **has** already **cut up** all the ingredients for the stir-fry.
>
> **7.** I**'ve finished** all my vegetables. May I please be excused now?
>
> **8.** How many times **have** I **told** you to eat with your mouth shut?

3 Match the example sentences in the box with their rules in the chart.

	The present perfect is used:	Signal Words
2	**a.** to talk about actions or states that started in the past and continue up to the present.	*for, since*
	b. to talk about things that happened at an unknown time before the present.	*already, still, yet*
	c. to talk about events that happened in the very recent past and relate to the present.	*just, recently, lately*
	d. to talk about states or actions that happened at an indefinite time in the past but relate to the present.	*always, before, ever, never, so far, up to now*
	e. to talk about actions or states that started in the past and stop at the present moment, commonly used with signal words.	*up to now, to the present time, so far*
	f. to talk about repeated actions or states that started in the past and stop at the present moment.	*how many times, how often, every day this week*

Like the present perfect, the present perfect progressive (*have/has* + *been* + present participle), links the past and the present. It is used to talk about actions that started in the past and continue right into the present. This is similar to the present perfect, but the progressive emphasizes the continuing nature of the action. It is also used to talk about actions that started in the past and are ongoing, and to talk about recently finished actions that have affected present circumstances.

The present perfect usually refers to a completed action, while the present perfect progressive emphasizes an unfinished action.

PRESENT PERFECT (finished actions)	**PRESENT PERFECT PROGRESSIVE** (unfinished actions)
I**'ve already** made the soup.	I**'ve been making** soup all morning.
I'm exhausted—I**'ve** just **baked** two batches of cookies.	I'm exhausted—I**'ve been baking** all morning.
Chef Miller **has created** prizewinning dishes for two decades.	Chef Miller **has been creating** prize-winning dishes for two decades.

4 Complete the passage with an appropriate form of the verb in parentheses. In some cases, more than one answer is possible. Then work with a partner and compare your answers.

People around the world (**1. enjoy**) _have been enjoying_ chocolate in many forms for hundreds of years. Originally begun by the Aztec Indians of Central America, the cultivation of cacao beans, from which chocolate is made, (**2. spread**) _____ around the equator. Cacao trees now (**3. provide**) _____ jobs and income for people from Africa, the Caribbean, Southeast Asia, and the South Pacific Islands of Samoa and New Guinea, to mention a few.

These days, the cultivation of cacao beans (**4. focus**) _____ on three main varieties of beans: Forastero, Criollo, and Trinitario. About 90 percent of the world's production (**5. come**) _____ from Forastero beans, the most common variety. The most popular variety, Criollo, (**6. possess**) _____ an especially prized aroma and taste. The best chocolate companies around the world (**7. compete**) _____ for these top-quality beans. The Trinitario variety (**8. be**) _____ the result of crossing Criollo and Forastero beans.

Whatever the variety of cacao beans used, people (**9. consume**) _____ chocolate in vast quantities.

5 **Check Your Understanding** Check the tenses you are likely to use in the situations. More than one may be used in some situations.

Situation	Simple Present	Present Progressive	Present Perfect
a. describing the dish you have on the stove to a friend			
b. describing the reasons why you eat what you do			
c. describing a favorite food experience			

 6 **Express Yourself** Work with a partner. Choose a situation from the chart. Write a dialogue and present it to another pair.

LISTENING and SPEAKING

Listen: Pizza Passion

1 **Before You Listen** What do you know about the origin of pizza? Do you like pizza? If so, what toppings do you like? If not, why not? How often do you eat pizza? On what occasions? Compare your answers with a partner's.

 Listening for Gist and Details When listening for understanding, effective listeners use different techniques for different purposes. When interested in a broad overview of a topic, they focus on the main idea. When they need details, they listen for specific information, such as dates, names, and so on.

  Listen and check the best summary of the main idea.

_____ **a.** The origins of pizza go back to the Greeks.

_____ **b.** Pizza was a favorite dish of Queen Margherita.

_____ **c.** Pizza has a long and impressive history.

3 Listen again, this time for details, and take notes to answer the following questions.

a. What classic civilization invented the forerunner of the pizza?

b. What city in Italy is the home of the modern pizza?

c. Who made the first pizza Margherita and why?

d. What are the ingredients in a pizza Margherita?

e. According to the rules established by the *Associazione Verace Pizza Napoletana*, what ingredients are allowed in dough?

f. When did pizza appear in the United States?

Pronunciation

Plural nouns in English end in –*s* or –*es*, as do present tense verbs in the third person singular. These endings have three different pronunciations: /s/, /z/, and /ɪz/.

	/s/	/z/	/ɪz/
Noun plurals	chocolates	apples	peaches
Verbs in third person singular	tastes	peels	slices

4 Work with a partner. Predict the pronunciation of the *–s* or *–es* endings of the underlined words.

The cooking of Nepal mixes elements of Asian, Indian, and Tibetan cuisines. Spices such as chile peppers, coriander seeds, fenugreek, and turmeric are found in many dishes. Popular foods include peas, lentils, potatoes, rice, carrots, tomatoes, and cucumbers. A person from Nepal typically drinks a Tibetan tea made with black tea, milk, butter, and salt.

5 Listen to the passage to check your predictions.

6 Work with a partner. Take turns reading the sentences aloud focusing on the *–s* and *–es* endings.

Speak Out

STRATEGY **Opening a Meeting or Discussion** At work or at school, people participate in meetings and discussions. These often follow predictable stages.

Stage	Sample Language
Greetings	Good morning, everyone. Thank you for coming. Good afternoon, Dr. Lange, Ms. Milton.
Introductions	At our meeting today, we have nutritionist Sarah Davidson. We also have . . . Why don't we introduce ourselves? I'll begin. I'm . . .
Stating the purpose	Today we'll cover the following items . . . Our goal this morning is to . . . and how to . . .
Setting the time frame	We have two hours to solve the problem, so . . . Our meeting is scheduled to last for one hour.
Opening the discussion	Mr. Carter, would you like to begin? Ms. Sawyer will start us off today.

7 Work in small groups. Choose topics for discussion. Take turns opening a discussion, following the stages above.

- Pica, a condition in which people consume non-food items, such as laundry starch, dirt, ice, and clay, is becoming popular in your area.
- Some people believe that your life is extended by seventy-five days for each new dish or food you taste.
- (your own idea)

Read About It

 Before You Read How much do you know about coffee? Take this short quiz and find out. Write **T** (true) or **F** (false) on the line.

_____ **1.** The word *coffee* once meant "wine."

_____ **2.** Americans, Germans, and Colombians account for fully 65 percent of the world's coffee consumption.

_____ **3.** Honoré de Balzac, the 19ᵗʰ century French writer, was so addicted to coffee that he drank up to 40 cups of coffee a day.

_____ **4.** The caffeine in coffee decreases blood flow throughout the body.

_____ **5.** Parents should never give coffee to children.

 Using Contextual Clues When reading for understanding, efficient readers try to figure out the meaning of unknown words from context. They look at several kinds of contextual clues: the part of speech of the unknown word; word parts such as *prefixes, word roots, suffixes;* words and sentences before and after the unknown word; possible synonyms and antonyms; and topic-related meanings that seem logical or plausible.

 Read the article. As you read, pay attention to context clues to guess meanings of unfamiliar words.

The World's Most Popular Beverage

Coffee is indeed the world's most popular drink—over 400 billion cups of coffee are happily consumed each year. So, just who is drinking all this coffee? People from every country around the world, certainly, even though the Americans, the French, and the Germans consume over 65 percent of the world's yearly production by themselves. According to where they are from and

5 their personal preference, coffee lovers the world over enjoy this aromatic beverage iced or steaming hot; black or with milk; with lemon peel or whipped cream; with spices such as cinnamon, ginger, or cardamom or with chocolate; with brandy or whiskey; and even with a pinch of salt or pepper. Coffee drinkers start

10 their day with it, drink it as a mid-morning pick-me-up, sip it after lunch, and linger over it after dinner and dessert.

The first coordinated attempt to cultivate the coffee plant was made on the Arabian peninsula around 1100 A.D. Arabs extracted the beans from the red coffee berries, roasted them, and then boiled them in water to make *qahwa*. By the 1500s,

15 coffee had taken hold all over the Middle East, and the world's first coffee shop was established in Constantinople. Coffee came to Europe through the port of Venice around 1600 and only seven years later was introduced to America by Captain John Smith, the founder of Virginia. The Dutch became the first to see the potential in transporting and cultivating coffee as a business in 1690, but they had to contend with smugglers, who secretly took coffee plants and seeds

20 to Brazil from Ceylon to sell. Many of the important coffee-producing countries owe their beginnings to those first smugglers.

For all practical purposes, coffee beans are of two types—Arabica and Robusta. As the name indicates, Arabica derives from the earliest cultivated species in the Middle East. Arabica beans cost more because they are highly prized for their rich flavor and aroma, and also because they
25 require a great amount of care to cultivate properly. Robusta, on the other hand, requires less care, and so grows more successfully in West Africa and Southeast Asia. It tolerates different climates better than Arabica and contains twice the caffeine of Arabica as well.

Unfortunately, the flavor and aroma of Robusta can't compare, and so it accounts for about 25 percent of the coffee grown around the world, while Arabica accounts for 75 percent.

30 As people consume more and more coffee, they wonder about its effect on their health. Coffee contains caffeine, an alkaloid compound also found in tea and cola nuts, among other products. Coffee drinkers worry that coffee might be addictive and that caffeine might have harmful effects. Studies have shown that caffeine does stimulate the central nervous system, as well as the cardiovascular system. It increases blood pressure up to a point and also increases
35 the secretion of gastric acid, thus aiding digestion. It is highly valued for its ability to make people feel more alert and less tired, and for that reason it is a favorite of students and office workers. It also helps fight migraine headaches, and for that reason may be a favorite of teachers and bosses! Measurement of caffeine varies according to the plant—a five-ounce cup of coffee made from Arabica beans will contain around 1.53 percent, while the same amount made from
40 Robusta beans will contain around 6 percent. Other factors that affect caffeine levels include the amount of coffee used and the method used to brew it. Most experts agree, however, that caffeine does not pose a danger if consumed in moderate amounts. So, friend, if you are a coffee drinker who is worrying about caffeine, relax. Have a "cuppa joe".

 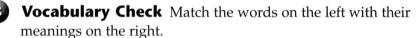 **Vocabulary Check** Match the words on the left with their meanings on the right.

_____ **1.** aromatic (line 6)   **a.** put off leaving because you don't want to leave

_____ **2.** beverage (line 6)   **b.** people who carry items secretly across borders

_____ **3.** linger (line 11)   **c.** with a distinctive, pleasant smell

_____ **4.** smugglers (lines 19 & 21)   **d.** a discharged fluid

_____ **5.** prized (line 24)   **e.** assigned to, credited with

_____ **6.** compound (line 31)   **f.** a drink other than water

_____ **7.** secretion (line 35)   **g.** valued as the best, appreciated

     h. a chemical substance, a combination

 Answer the questions. Compare your answers with a partner's.

a. What are several ways that coffee is served?

b. What is the origin of coffee?

c. What are the two main types of coffee beans, and what are their characteristics?

d. What are some of the physical effects of coffee?

Think About It

 5 What is the role of coffee in social situations? If you are a coffee drinker, what are your own habits regarding coffee?

Wanda was proud of herself for sticking to her one-cup-a-day limit...

Write: Review of Paragraph Structure

STRATEGY Effective writing has a specific topic, audience, and purpose. Each paragraph presents a main idea that appears in a topic sentence at the beginning or end of the paragraph. At times, the main idea might be implied rather than stated directly. Effective paragraphs also contain supporting sentences that develop the main idea, and often use transitional expressions (*for example, however, also, as a result,* etc.) to relate ideas to each other.

Once you know how to write a good paragraph, it is easy to understand the organizational structure of an essay. An essay is made up of paragraphs about a single topic and contains three sections:

- An introduction containing a thesis statement, which states the main idea of the essay.
- Body paragraphs, which give details and other information to support the thesis statement.
- A conclusion, which summarizes the main point and brings the essay to an end.

Write About It

 6 Choose a topic from the box below, and write a short essay. Before writing, identify your purpose (e.g., to give information, to express an opinion), your main idea, and your audience. Remember your purpose and main idea should be closely related. As you write, be sure to use topic sentences, supporting sentences, and transitional expressions.

• Eat Raw Foods for Better Health	• All Foods—But in Moderation
• A Favorite Holiday Meal	• (your own idea)

  7 **Check Your Writing** Exchange papers with a partner. Use the questions below to give feedback to your partner. When you get your own paper back, revise as necessary.

- Are the purpose and main idea clear?
- Is the essay suitable for its audience?
- Is the main idea developed with supporting paragraphs?
- Are transitional expressions used?

FIRST CAR

MEMORABLE MOMENTS

Unit 2

GETTING STARTED

Warm Up

The Apollo XI moon landing, a teenager's first date, the splitting of the atom, the day you started school—all of these events are memorable, either on a personal or a world level. They are defining moments in our lives.

1 Make a list of the three most significant events in your life. Work in small groups. Describe these events and discuss how they affected you.

2 What were some important "world firsts"? What has their effect on the world been?

3 Listen to two friends talk about a survey on the most important events of the 20th century. List the three events they mention. Do you agree with the survey? Why or why not?

EVENT 1: _____

EVENT 2: _____

EVENT 3: _____

Figure It Out

4 Read one of the passages below and fill in the chart on page 17.
Work in groups of three. Take turns telling each other about your
reading passage. While listening, complete the chart.

Momentous "Firsts"

Student One

On May 29, 1953, Edmund Hillary of New Zealand and Tenzing
Norgay of Nepal became the first human beings to ascend Mount
Everest. Known as Chomolungma to the local people, it stands at
29,028 ft. (8,848 m) and is the highest place on earth… Neither
5 geography nor scientific progress was furthered by this achievement, yet
Hillary and Norgay instantly became heroes. This was in part because
they were men of heroic mold, but chiefly it was because they
represented the spirit of their time…

They were both very straightforward men. At the time, Tenzing was a professional
10 mountaineer from the Sherpa community in the Everest foothills, and New Zealander
Hillary was a beekeeper… Yet they both became representatives of the small nations of the
world, the tucked-away and up-and-coming countries…

Both men were showered with worldly honors, and they accepted them with style. Both
became the most celebrated citizens of their countries and went around the world on behalf
15 of them. Additionally, both devoted much of their lives to ensuring the happiness of the
Sherpas, Tenzing's people, true natives of the Everest region.

Student Two

…From childhood, Akio Morita had been destined to head the family
business at a prominent sake-brewing company in Nagoya. However,
he traded his life of comfort and privilege for the uncertainties of his
20 own start-up company, Sony, which later became a world leader in
electronics…

One of Sony's first products was a miniature transistor radio,
produced in 1955. The radio's success led to new inventions, such as
an 8-inch television and a videotape recorder.

25 The creation of the name Sony shows Morita's determination to communicate globally.
He wanted a name that was recognizable everywhere… It had to be creative, short, and
catchy. Morita and his partner Masaru Ibuka liked the word *sonus,* which means "sound" in
Latin. The word *sonny* was popular in the U.S. at the time, and they thought it suggested a
company of young people with abundant energy. The two words combined formed Sony…

30 The Walkman is one of Sony's most popular inventions. Morita came up with the idea
when he noticed people listening to music in their cars and carrying large stereos to the
beach and in the park. Morita insisted on a product that sounded like a high-quality car
stereo, yet was portable and allowed the user to listen while doing something else, like
walking. Thus was born the Walkman, a product which became a worldwide hit…

Student Three

35   In 1993, when the winner of the Nobel Prize for Literature was
announced, Toni Morrison never expected to hear her name called.
Despite six brilliant novels and a Pulitzer Prize, Morrison was shocked to
learn that she had become the first African-American and the eighth
woman ever to receive literature's most prestigious honor. "I guess there
40 are some people out there who like to hear my stories," the author said.

Toni Morrison was born in 1931, in Lorain, Ohio. She was part of a large family with a
vital sense of its heritage and a strong tradition of storytelling. Morrison's childhood was spent
absorbing language and stories from people around her—the women washing clothes and
cooking meals, and the old people swapping tall tales. She developed the sensitivity to
45 language that would play a large role in her fiction.

She later relocated to New York City. While she was working as an editor, she noticed
the lack of books by or about black women. She realized that she couldn't find the
counterparts of her extended family back home anywhere in fiction.

Morrison set out to change that. Few American authors have been as adept as Morrison
50 at capturing life on the page.

	Edmund Hillary & Tenzing Norgay	**Akio Morita**	**Toni Morrison**
Personal or World "First"			
Important Dates			
Biographical Information			
Other Important Information			

☑ **5** **Vocabulary Check** Match the words on the left with their meanings on the right.

_____ **1.** straightforward (line 9)
_____ **2.** start-up (line 20)
_____ **3.** catchy (line 27)
_____ **4.** thus (line 34)
_____ **5.** tall tale (line 44)
_____ **6.** counterparts (line 48)
_____ **7.** set out (line 49)

a. interesting, attracting attention
b. an exciting, often imaginary story
c. equivalent in function and characteristics
d. honest, without pretense
e. begin, undertake
f. newly created
g. businesslike
h. therefore, and so

Talk About It

 6 Work with a partner. Take turns interviewing each other about various important moments in your lives. Use the conversation below as a model.

Example: one defining moment in your life

ROLES	MODEL CONVERSATION	FUNCTIONS
Student:	So, what was one of the defining moments in your life?	Ask about past events.
Professor:	Well, I was living in Iran in 1979 during the revolution, and I remember very clearly when the shah left the country.	Give information about a past event.
Student:	Wow! What was it like?	Ask for more information.
Professor:	Well, on the one hand, I was worried about my future as an American in Iran. But on the other hand, it was a great lesson in modern history.	Elaborate.
Student:	That must have been amazing!	Make an assessment.

GRAMMAR

The Simple Past and Past Progressive Tenses

The simple past and past progressive tenses are used to talk about actions in the past. We can use the simple past for actions that were completed at a specific time in the past or for recurring actions in the past. The past progressive usually indicates an action that was ongoing at a specific time.

> I **ran** in the New York City Marathon in 1992. At the time, I **was working** for a company in New Jersey. When I was in high school, I **ran** in the marathon every year.

When is usually followed by the simple form of the verb; *while* is usually followed by a progressive form of the verb.

> 1. When I **lost** my job at the newspaper, I **decided** to become a novelist.
> 2. While we **were waiting** for the results of the entrance exam, we **were discussing** the chances we had of passing.
> 3. I **was waiting** tables at a café in Paris when I first **met** Pablo Picasso.

1 Match the example sentences from the box on page 18 with their rules below.

_____ **a.** The past progressive in both clauses is used with two actions, of equal importance and duration. They indicate the actions were in progress at the same time.

_____ **b.** The simple past in both clauses generally indicates that one action happened before the other.

_____ **c.** The past progressive with the simple past shows that an action was the background for another, or that an action was interrupted by another. The action in progress (past progressive) is the background for the completed action (simple past).

2 Read these statements about Joseph Pulitzer and the Pulitzer Prize. Correct the mistakes in the sentences that follow them.

Example: Joseph Pulitzer emigrated from Hungary to the U.S. in 1864 and served in a cavalry regiment until the end of the Civil War.

    • Pulitzer served in a cavalry regiment in ~~Hungary~~. _the U.S._

a. While he was studying law, he participated in politics.

    • He participated in politics and then became a law student.

b. After working for some time in New York sweatshops, the young Pulitzer went west and became a reporter.

    • Pulitzer worked in sweatshops after he went west.

c. He established himself as a journalist and began to build his newspaper publishing empire.

    • He was establishing himself as a journalist when he began to build his newspaper publishing empire.

d. Joseph Pulitzer was thinking of his place in history when he conceived of the Pulitzer Prize.

    • He already knew his place in history before he thought up the prize.

3 Work with a partner. Think of several world events that have happened during your lifetime. Talk about what you were doing when those events took place.

Example: _I was watching the morning news when I first heard about the Kobe earthquake._

The Past Perfect Tense

To show that a past action was completed before another or before a specific time in the past, we often use the past perfect tense. We typically use the past perfect with *when, by the time, already, after,* and *before.*

The past perfect is not necessary if *before* or *after* appears in the sentence, because the time relationship is clear. The simple past may be used with both verbs.

> By the time I **got** my degree, I **had** already **changed** my mind about my career.
>
> Before Morita **invented** the Walkman, he **created** the videotape recorder.
>
> After he **had achieved** his original goals, he **began** to look for new challenges.
> OR
> After he **achieved** his original goals, he **began** to look for new challenges.

4 The timeline below gives you important events in the life of golf legend Tiger Woods. Using the timeline, complete the sentences with the appropriate form of the verb.

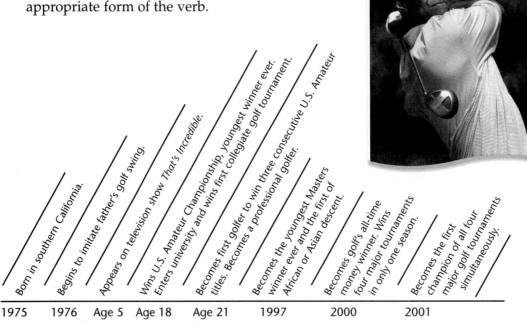

Born in southern California.

Begins to imitate father's golf swing.

Appears on television show *That's Incredible.*

Wins U.S. Amateur Championship, youngest winner ever. Enters university and wins first collegiate golf tournament.

Becomes first golfer to win three consecutive U.S. Amateur titles. Becomes a professional golfer.

Becomes the youngest Masters winner ever and the first of African or Asian descent.

Becomes golf's all-time money winner. Wins four major tournaments in only one season.

Becomes the first champion of all four major golf tournaments simultaneously.

| 1975 | 1976 | Age 5 | Age 18 | Age 21 | 1997 | 2000 | 2001 |

Example: By the age of six months, Tiger Woods **(discover)** <u>had already discovered</u> golf.

a. While he **(watch)** _____ his father hit golf balls, be **(begin)** _____ to imitate him.

b. Then, at the age of 18, Tiger Woods **(become)** _____ the youngest U.S. Amateur Champion in golf history.

c. While he **(study)** _____ at Stanford University, he **(win)** _____ his first collegiate golf tournament.

d. By the time he **(turn)** _____ 21, he **(win)** _____ three consecutive U.S. Amateur titles.

e. In 1997, he **(become)** _____ the youngest Masters winner ever and the first of African or Asian descent.

f. By 2000, he **(earn)** _____ more money than any other player in golf history.

5 Make a timeline with the dates of five significant events in your life, but do not write the events. Exchange timelines with a partner. Take turns guessing what events might have happened on those dates.

6 **Check Your Understanding** Write a few sentences on each topic below. Use the verb tenses in parentheses.

a. first day of school (_simple past_)
b. earliest childhood memories (_simple past_)
c. development of the Web (_simple past and past perfect_)
d. the life of a celebrity (_simple past and past progressive_)

7 **Express Yourself** Work with a partner. Take turns reading aloud your sentences from the exercise above. Ask and answer questions about them.

LISTENING and SPEAKING

Listen: Bungee Jumping and Whitewater Rafting

1 **Before You Listen** You will hear people talking about two personal firsts: bungee jumping and whitewater rafting. What do you know about these two extreme sports? Discuss your answers in small groups.

STRATEGY **Listening for Sequence** When you are listening for understanding, it is important to understand the order in which the events occurred. To establish a sequence of events, listen for time expressions such as _first_, _second_, _then_, _next_, and _finally_.

2 Listen to a conversation among three friends. As you listen, number the events below in the order they happened. Compare your answers with a partner's.

Bungee Jumping	Whitewater Rafting
____ Stepped on the platform	____ Learned to paddle in unison
____ Had his weight checked	____ Was pulled back into the raft
____ Signed a waiver form	____ Got into the raft
____ Had the bungee cord wrapped around his legs	____ Fell into the river
	____ Put on wet suits

3 Listen to the conversation again. This time, identify the emotions the two people went through. Compare your answers with a partner's.

4 Work in small groups. Do you have any personal firsts involving risk that are similar to those in the conversation? Tell your group about them.

Pronunciation

> **Pronunciation Changes in Final -ed**
>
> The -*d*/-*ed* endings of past tense verbs are often pronounced /t/,/d/, or/ɪd/
>
> Each spring, the local priest bless**ed** the fishing boats before they sail**ed** for the first time. Many villagers participat**ed** in the event.
>
> However, when some verbs are used as *adjectives*, the pronunciation is always /ɪd/:
>
> A bless**ed** event   A learn**ed** man   A want**ed** criminal

5 Work with a partner. Decide if the boldface words below are used as verbs or adjectives. Predict the sound of –*ed* by checking the appropriate column.

	/d/	/t/	/ɪd/
a. Edison **invented** the first phonograph in 1878.			
b. The numbers for the company's first-year profits look like **invented** figures; they couldn't have earned that much.			
c. Becoming a mother for the first time was the most important event in my life, and I **learned** a lot about the responsibilities of being a parent.			
d. Many famous inventors were not **learned** men and women; their education was practical rather than formal.			

6 Listen to the sentences to check your predictions.

7 Work with a partner. Take turns reading the sentences focusing on the -*ed* endings.

Speak Out

Defining an Issue Formal discussions usually follow a set structure. After the leader opens the discussion, the participants usually define the issue in order to make sure that everyone has the same understanding of the problem before moving on to further discussion.

Defining the Issue

As I see it, the real issue here is . . .

When I say . . . I mean . . .

Now when I speak of . . . I'm talking about . . ., . . ., . . .

---

8 Work in groups to define the italicized words in the issues below.

  a. There has been an increase in *vandalism* in your community. A number of local students have been caught committing such acts.

  b. Children are spending more time using computers at school and less time working with others. As a result, they have poor *social skills*.

READING and WRITING

Read About It

1 **Before You Read** Work in small groups and discuss the questions.

  a. What are some world firsts in engineering? In your opinion, which has had the greatest impact on humanity?

  b. What are some world firsts in aviation? Again, which has had the biggest impact on humanity?

Reading for Time Organization Readers can improve their understanding by noting the sequence of events. Time expressions such as *first, second, then, next,* and *finally* help us to identify the stages in a process or event; actual dates and times help us to establish the overall time frame; and words such as *while* and *when* help us to understand the connection between different events within a sentence. Look for chronological information as you read the article on pages 24-25.

PAUL MACCREADY'S FLYING CIRCUS

by Mark Wheeler

Striding into his office on a June afternoon, a slightly rumpled-looking Paul MacCready juggles an armful of folders with a bag of take-out Thai food and apologizes for his tardiness. "I was up until 3 A.M. the past few nights working on some projects," he explains, fidgeting with

5 his glasses as he drops the folders, his lunch, and then himself on the couch. What sort of projects? The gray-haired, seventy-four-year-old company founder hesitates. But then his enthusiasm gets the better of him.

10 "I may have found a way to make exercise addictive," he says, launching into an energetic description of his "Micro Gym," a pocket-size exercise machine with a pulse meter that vibrates when the user reaches an optimal

15 heart rate. "Just enough exercise to get that rush of endorphins that will make you want to do it again," says MacCready. "Wouldn't that be a great service to humanity?"

From anyone else, the idea might seem pure fantasy. But MacCready has a knack for making the fantastic real. In 1977, the mild-mannered aeronautical engineer

20 designed the first plane powered solely by human effort — a furiously pedaling pilot — capable of sustained flight. Dubbed the *Gossamer Condor*, the flying machine now sits alongside the Wright Brothers' *Flyer* and Charles Lindbergh's *Spirit of St. Louis* in the Smithsonian's Air and Space Museum.

MacCready grew up in New Haven, Connecticut, where his father was a doctor

25 and his mother a nurse. Shy and diminutive, he spent his free hours immersing himself in his hobbies —- collecting moths and butterflies and collecting model airplanes. "I think kids do better if they have a hobby, a topic they know better than anybody else," he says. By his early teens, MacCready had begun building flying machines, and by age sixteen, he had followed them into the sky as a licensed pilot. "That really gave

30 me confidence in myself," he recalls. MacCready was even more thrilled when he was introduced to the sport of soaring — glider flying — at age twenty. "Unlike with conventional aircraft, this was pure, quiet, birdlike flight," he says. "It was my first insight into how technology could be combined with the natural world."

In 1957, MacCready wed Judy Leonard, the daughter of one of his soaring

35 colleagues, and he set about launching an engineering career. "I didn't want to join a standard aerospace firm, the kind that buys engineers by the acre," he says. "Such places foster by-the-book thinking, a lockstep way of approaching a problem." Instead, MacCready started Meteorology Research Inc., a business specializing in flying small planes into clouds to try to modify the amount of rainfall they would produce. When it

40 worked, says MacCready, "it was fun, it gave me a feeling of omnipotence. We got pretty good at creating lightning, but there wasn't much of a market for it." MacCready left the company in 1970 and soon after began AeroVironment to develop renewable energy sources like wind and solar power, a mission close to his heart. "We are quickly using up the resources of a finite planet," he says.

45 But the inspiration for his most noted achievements, the Gossamer projects, came from less lofty ambitions. In the early 1970s, a relative had to default on a business

loan, and MacCready, who had co-signed the note, suddenly found himself owing $100,000. While searching for a way to pay it back, he recalled an eighteen-year-old challenge that had been offered by British industrialist Henry Kremet to the first person
50 who could complete a 1.15-mile-long figure-eight course using human-powered flight. The prize? $100,000. "All the conventional ways to achieve human flight had been tried," MacCready says. "People were stuck."

A solution came to MacCready as he was driving cross-country on vacation with Judy and their three sons, and started watching the hawks and turkey vultures soaring in
55 circles overhead, taking advantage of updrafts. He got to thinking about the size and weight of the birds, and how much power for each pound of weight an animal — or an airplane — needed to fly. "That's when the great 'Aha!' moment hit," he says. "I realized that as long as you kept the weight the same, you could take an airplane and let the wings get bigger and bigger. The flight speed would decrease, but so would the power
60 needed to make the plane fly." MacCready wasn't looking for speed. He just wanted to reduce the necessary power enough so that a single human being could complete the Kremer challenge.

Back in his office, MacCready and his colleagues set out to prove that theory with the *Gossamer Condor*. They designed a light plane and MacCready drafted his sons, then
65 teenagers, as test pilots. "They were the right size — small, lightweight," says Judy. "And we didn't have to pay them anything." Ultimately, the *Condor* met Kremer's challenge — and made aviation history!

2 On a separate sheet of paper, list events that happened at these points in Paul's life.

• childhood	• age 20	• 1970
• age 16	• 1957	• 1977

 3 **Vocabulary Check** Match the words on the left with their meanings on the right.

_____ **1.** fidget (line 4)
_____ **2.** knack (line 18)
_____ **3.** immerse oneself (line 25)
_____ **4.** soar (lines 31 and 34)
_____ **5.** insight (line 33)
_____ **6.** by-the-book (line 37)
_____ **7.** lofty (line 46)

a. with high principles
b. clear understanding
c. interrupted
d. move nervously
e. conventional, following the rules
f. natural ability
g. fly effortlessly
h. become absorbed

Think About It

4 On a scale of 1 to 10, how important is a human-powered plane? What would be its impact on the world? Discuss your answer with a partner.

Write: Analyzing Essay Questions

Most academic writing is either persuasive or descriptive. A persuasive essay may contain some description, but its main purpose is to present the writer's opinion and convince the reader to adopt it. Similarly, a descriptive essay may present some of the writer's opinions on the topic, but its main purpose is to inform the reader about objective facts.

 STRATEGY When you are taking an essay test, the questions will determine your essay's purpose. Read the questions carefully, looking for key words that will help you decide whether the overall purpose is persuasion or description.

5 Decide if each essay question is asking for a **P** (persuasive) or a **D** (descriptive) essay. Circle the words in the question that helped you decide.

> ESSAY QUESTIONS
>
> _____ 1. The invention of the sewing machine had a great impact. What were some sociological changes brought about by this machine? Refer to specific examples in your answer.
>
> _____ 2. Awards and prizes are given for excellence in various fields. Choose one major award, and discuss how the recipients are selected and the potential impact of the award on the recipient's career.
>
> _____ 3. Do you agree or disagree with the following statement? "Successes and failures in childhood have lasting psychological effects on us." Support your answer by referring to specific examples.
>
> _____ 4. Some say that the fall of the Berlin Wall was the most important event of the 20th century. Others make the same claim for the abolition of apartheid in South Africa. Which event do you think was more significant, and why?

Write About It

6 Write three to four paragraphs on one of the essay questions.

  7 **Check Your Writing** Work in small groups. Read your paragraphs. Ask the group members to identify the paragraphs' purpose. Use the questions below to give feedback and revise as necessary.

> • Does each paragraph have a topic sentence?
> • Are time words used to signal the sequence of events?
> • Are different verb tenses used correctly?
> • What could be changed to make the paragraphs clearer?

GETTING STARTED

Warm Up

Many things have changed since the appearance of the first black and white silent movies: sound and color have been added, computerized animation and special effects have been developed, and 35mm film is being replaced by digital images.

1 What do you think the cinema of the future will be like?

2 Listen to three friends discuss what makes *Citizen Kane* so exceptional. Fill in the chart. Then compare your answers with a partner's.

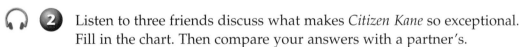

Story	Direction	Acting	Photography

Figure It Out

 Margo Rogers is a reporter for the *Daily Word* newspaper. She is interviewing Harjiv Kalbag, president of Digital Solutions, a company specializing in digital technology.

MARGO: Harjiv, what changes can we expect in filmmaking as a result of digital technology?

HARJIV: Well, new digital cinema's being developed. It'll provide the motion picture industry with new capabilities, superior quality, and opportunities for new business.

MARGO: Sorry, let me stop you for a moment. Just what *is* digital cinema exactly?

HARJIV: Oh! Digital cinema is a system which delivers motion pictures to theaters throughout the world using digital technology, such as DVD or satellite. So, instead of reels of film going into the theaters, movies will be transmitted via satellite.

MARGO: OK. But could you be a little more specific? How will all this work?

HARJIV: Sure. Transmitting movies by satellite is going to work something like this: A studio turns a completed movie over to a company. The company scans and digitizes each frame, and turns the film into a gigantic computer file.

MARGO: I see.

HARJIV: And once this is done, you see, the movie—now a big data file— is compressed and encrypted. Then it's sent by satellite to a regional hub which can transmit the movie to any number of cinemas. There'll be no more shipping, no more spools, or splicing together multiple reels of film. So, the distribution and transmission of movies will be much cheaper, easier, and faster.

MARGO: What about the movie audiences? How will they be affected by all this?

HARJIV: They've actually got a lot to gain. The digital cinema is going to give audiences pristine digital images and sound at every showing, no matter how often it's shown. Also, the images on the screen will be stable, with no more film scratches, dirt, burns, or splices.

MARGO: That sounds great! I can't wait to see a movie like that!

HARJIV: If you're interested, I'm meeting several film industry CEOs to have an experimental screening tomorrow. Why don't you join us?

MARGO: Absolutely! I'm very interested! Where? When?

HARJIV: The screening starts at 11 A.M. at the Star Movie Theatre. See you there then?

MARGO: Thanks. I can't wait!

Vocabulary Check Match the words on the left with their meanings on the right.

_____	**1.** deliver (line 8)	**a.** coded
_____	**2.** encrypted (line 19)	**b.** showing of a film
_____	**3.** hub (line 20)	**c.** unspoiled, clean
_____	**4.** spool (line 21)	**d.** quality
_____	**5.** pristine (line 26)	**e.** distribution center
_____	**6.** screening (lines 31 & 33)	**f.** device around which tape, film, cotton, etc. is wound
		g. carry and distribute

Talk About It

 A reporter is interviewing a film industry expert about the future of moviemaking. Work with a partner. Take turns being the reporter and the film expert and discuss the topics below. Use the conversation as a model.

Example: the role of 35 mm film

ROLES	MODEL CONVERSATION	FUNCTIONS
Reporter:	What role will the 35mm film have in the movie industry in fifty years?	Ask for a prediction.
Expert:	In my opinion, it is going to disappear.	Make a prediction.
Reporter:	How come? Why is that?	Ask for a reason.
Expert:	Because new technologies are surely going to make it obsolete.	Give a reason.

<u>Topics</u>

a. single-film movie theatres

b. special effects

c. global popularity of American movies

d. salaries of actors

e. movie camera technology

f. (your own idea)

GRAMMAR

Going to, Will, Present Progressive, and Simple Present

We can use *going to, will,* the present progressive, and the simple present to talk about the future.

Going to and *will* are both used to make predictions or express future intention. *Going to* expresses an intention based on people's plans or decisions in the present. *Will* expresses a definite belief about the future.

> I believe that digital filmmaking **will** be very common in fifty years.
>
>   (a belief that this will be a fact in the future)
>
> All the experts say that digital video cameras **are going to be** very cheap in five years.
>
>   (a prediction based on information in the present)

The simple present and present progressive can be used to describe future actions that are definitely arranged or planned. They can also be used to talk about scheduled future events such as timetables and programs. The simple present form expresses a statement of fact. The progressive emphasizes the action, its current importance, or a change of plan.

> The movie **starts** at 7:30. It says so in the paper.
>
> We'**re meeting** at the theater at seven, not at 6:30.

1 Read the article. Underline all the verbs that have a future meaning. Compare your answers with a partner's and discuss.

Virtual Reality

Imagine a friend of yours calling you and saying, "Sorry! I can't make it to the party. I'm playing in the NBA with Michael Jordan, and the game starts at 7 P.M. tonight. I'll tell you all about it later." Your friend of course would not be a basketball superstar, just a Virtual Reality (VR) fan.

With the help of computers, VR technology can create an altered reality by sending information to the senses. For a VR participant, real and virtual reality become intermingled.

Today VR systems rely heavily on visual stimulation to create the illusion of reality. However, judging from current experiments, sound, touch, and even smell are soon going to be much more part of the VR experience. As better technology becomes readily available, it is going to become impossible to tell the difference between true reality and its virtual equivalent. We have microprocessors that can be connected directly to the optical nerve, 3-D surround-sound, and touch sensitive body suits that will revolutionize entertainment as we know it. Soon, we will be able to do things in VR we can't do in real life: we will be able to fly, jump off Niagara Falls, and climb up skyscrapers. With the new VR, not even the sky will be the limit!

Of course the best way of achieving a total sense of reality is connecting a computer to the human brain and stimulating the senses directly. When this is achieved, it will provide a perfect virtual reality experience without all the clumsy equipment currently in use.

Some say that the most exciting form of virtual entertainment would be to build an entire virtual world. In the future, it seems likely that we will not only spend more time with computers but live in them too!

2 Complete the sentences with the most appropriate form of the verb in parentheses. Compare your answers with a partner's.

1. **A:** What was the Cannes film festival like this year?
   B: It was inspiring to see all these young, talented directors. And it was interesting that so many of them were Mexicans.
   A: Yes, I predict Mexican cinema **(be)** _____ world-famous soon.
   B: I agree, especially with these recent films.

2. **A:** Do you want to come over on Saturday evening?
   B: Sorry, but I **(watch)** _____ the Oscars on Saturday night.
   A: Oh, come on. You can videotape it.
   B: OK. I **(visit)** _____ you instead.

3. **A:** Come on! We're **(be)** _____ late, I'm afraid.
   B: What time _____ the movie **(start)** _____?
   A: At 8:30. And it's already eight o'clock!

3 Circle the form that best completes each sentence in the e-mail. Compare your answers with a partner's and explain your choices.

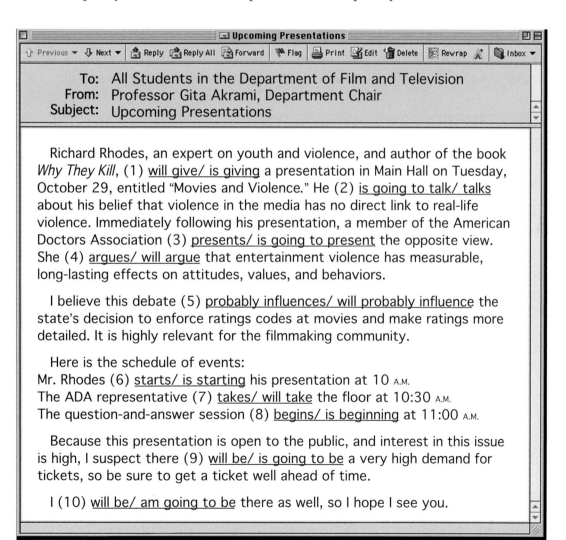

To: All Students in the Department of Film and Television
From: Professor Gita Akrami, Department Chair
Subject: Upcoming Presentations

Richard Rhodes, an expert on youth and violence, and author of the book *Why They Kill*, (1) will give/ is giving a presentation in Main Hall on Tuesday, October 29, entitled "Movies and Violence." He (2) is going to talk/ talks about his belief that violence in the media has no direct link to real-life violence. Immediately following his presentation, a member of the American Doctors Association (3) presents/ is going to present the opposite view. She (4) argues/ will argue that entertainment violence has measurable, long-lasting effects on attitudes, values, and behaviors.

I believe this debate (5) probably influences/ will probably influence the state's decision to enforce ratings codes at movies and make ratings more detailed. It is highly relevant for the filmmaking community.

Here is the schedule of events:
Mr. Rhodes (6) starts/ is starting his presentation at 10 A.M.
The ADA representative (7) takes/ will take the floor at 10:30 A.M.
The question-and-answer session (8) begins/ is beginning at 11:00 A.M.

Because this presentation is open to the public, and interest in this issue is high, I suspect there (9) will be/ is going to be a very high demand for tickets, so be sure to get a ticket well ahead of time.

I (10) will be/ am going to be there as well, so I hope I see you.

☑ ④ Check Your Understanding Check the future forms that you are *most likely* to use in the situations below. Compare your answers with a partner's.

SITUATION	will	going to	present progressive	simple present
a. predicting the effects of a big media event, such as a presidential visit, on your town	☐	☐	☐	☐
b. speculating about the career of a well-known actor in your country	☐	☐	☐	☐
c. talking about new TV channels available on satellite TV	☐	☐	☐	☐
d. presenting the show times at a multiplex cinema	☐	☐	☐	☐

⑤ Express Yourself Work with a partner. Choose one of the situations and write a dialogue. Practice your dialogue and then act it out for another pair.

LISTENING and SPEAKING

Listen: The Future of Movies

① Before you Listen Professional-quality digital cameras and editing software are becoming more affordable. How do you think this will affect the movie industry? Discuss your ideas in small groups.

STRATEGY ▶ Listening Critically Listening critically often means listening for both the strengths and weaknesses of arguments. When you listen, it is important to listen for key supporting information to evaluate how strong the argument is.

**② ** Listen to a panel of experts giving their predictions about the future of the film industry. Check the predictions below that you hear discussed.

☐ **a.** In the future, more people will be able to make movies.
☐ **b.** Moviemakers will need a lot of money to make films in the future.
☐ **c.** The market for movies will be completely filled.
☐ **d.** There will always be an audience for quality films.
☐ **e.** Anyone with a camera will be able to make a quality film.
☐ **f.** Digital movies will bring an end to all censorship.
☐ **g.** Not all censorship is bad.

3 Choose one prediction from page 32. Listen again and note the supporting evidence. Then work with a partner and compare notes.

a. How many supporting reasons were given? Were these reasons strong or weak? Explain why you think so.

b. Discuss one or more of these opinions in small groups. Do you agree or disagree with the opinion? Give support for your opinion.

Pronunciation

> **Two-Syllable Words with Two Stress Patterns**
>
> Some two-syllable words are pronounced differently according to their part of speech.
>
> They are stressed on the first syllable when they are nouns and stressed on the second syllable when they are verbs.
>
> **A:** Orson Welles went against established norms of cinematography in making *Citizen Kane*. In his day he was a real **RE•bel.**
>
> **B:** That's right. And now lots of young directors **re•BEL** against the status quo.

4 Look at the sentences in the box.

- What part of speech is the word rebel in the first sentence?
- What part of speech is the word rebel in the second sentence?

5 Predict the stress of the underlined words. Put an accent mark (´) on the stressed syllable.

The film *Orfeu* is a <u>remake</u> of the 1958 Oscar-winning classic *Black Orpheus*. In the modern-day *Orfeu*, filmmaker Carlos Diegues <u>permits</u> us to enter the slums of Rio to observe the lives of two lovers who are ultimately caught in a <u>conflict</u> between rival drug gangs that rule their world. The film <u>contrasts</u> the lives of its two main characters, the mythical musician Orpheus, played by Brazilian singer Toni Garrido, and the childhood friend of Orpheus who has become the slum's ruthless druglord. Orpheus and the residents of the slums must contend with an <u>increase</u> in violence from a police force that cannot cope with the heavily armed gangs. The violence <u>progresses</u> until ultimately no one is safe. The film's escalation of violence continues until the tragic climax set against the samba rhythms of Rio's Carnaval.

Listen to the film synopsis to check your predictions.

 Work with a partner. Take turns reading sentences from the synopsis focusing on the syllable stress of the underlined words.

Speak Out

 Speaking Persuasively To convince others of your point of view, you need to present your ideas persuasively. You can do this by using supporting facts as evidence and/or by getting your listeners to agree with you on important points and then leading them to a logical conclusion. You also need to be able to politely point out the problems with opposing viewpoints. When speaking against an idea, you can either directly contradict what the other person has said or make concessions, agreeing with some of the reasoning but not with the main point. Making concessions is less confrontational.

SPEAKING FOR A POSITION	SPEAKING AGAINST A POSITION
Offering Evidence	**Contradicting**
The fact is that...	Not at all...
The facts show that...	Quite the opposite...
Getting Agreement	Actually, that's not quite accurate/true...
You have to admit that...	**Making Concessions**
You must agree that...	Yes, but still,...
Don't you think/agree that...?	Maybe so, but...
Clearly, ...	Even so,...
You can't deny that...	Even if that's true,...
Most authorities/experts agree that...	You have a point, but...
	Yes, but some maintain that...

 Read the situation below and roles on page 35. Brainstorm reasons to support each position. Work in small groups: one person will speak for the policy, one person will speak against the policy, and the third person will act as judge. The judges will decide whose presentation was more convincing.

> **SITUATION**
>
> You are on the board of directors of a movie production company .
> There have been many complaints by politicians and civic organizations about the extremely violent content of many of your company's movies. However, the most violent movies were the ones that brought in the most profit. You must decide on the type of movies your company will produce in the future.

ROLE A

Speaking for the company policy: You want to continue producing violent action movies, because there's a big market for them. With these movies, the company will surely make a profit for its shareholders. You believe that movie violence does not lead to real-life violence.

ROLE B

Speaking against the company policy: You want to change your company's policy, because you believe that violent movies have a negative effect on young viewers. As a consequence, you are afraid first-rate actors and directors will not want to work with you.

READING and WRITING

Read About It

1 **Before You Read** Work in small groups. List the five most important characteristics of a good actor. Share your ideas with other groups.

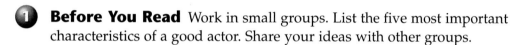 **Reading Critically** Reading critically means assessing the strengths and weaknesses of written positions. To do this, you need to be able to note and evaluate supporting information for each key idea.

2 Read the article. As you read, pay attention to the supporting details in each paragraph.

Virtual Actors Cause High Anxiety in Hollywood

Until recently, actors felt secure that they would never have to worry about being replaced by a digital counterpart. Their performances were thought to involve expression of complex emotions far too subtle to be replicated by a computer. However, because of a new digital technology known as photo-realistic animation, all
5 of that may change. Hollywood is abuzz with talk about how this new digital technique would enable filmmakers to create virtual actors that they hope will be as convincing as actual actors.

Needless to say, the actors themselves are not thrilled with this innovation. In fact, many actors are deeply troubled at the idea. The Screen Actors Guild, the leading
10 union for television and film actors, has issued a warning to filmmakers that it will be monitoring producer's activities closely for any signs that an actor's painstakingly prepared performances have been altered or even replaced by computer animation.

Why would film producers seriously consider using these virtual actors when big-name stars usually translate into success at the box-office? Simple—money. The
15 virtual actor will in effect be a digital robot who will do anything the producer desires, at any time, and at any place, without a whimper, or, without receiving a salary. The prospect of using hassle-free actors who need no contract, no sick days,

(continued on next page)

and who could be asked at any time to promote or endorse anything has many producers and directors overjoyed. And of course any profit these virtual actors made on films and endorsements would be going directly to the producer. Filmmakers believe they will save millions of dollars on the filming alone. And with the possibility of digital distribution included, it's no wonder that they are excited.

In fact, top directors have already used completely digital characters in films, such as Jar Jar Binks, a virtual character in *Star Wars: Episode 1 – The Phantom Menace*. However, many people think that only the fact that Jar Jar Binks was not a human, gave Lucas the freedom to use a digital character. The majority of people don't think it's possible to use computer animation to completely create a believable human character. The subtleties of a real actor's performance cannot be easily reproduced by animation experts. Many question the idea that digital performers really threaten actors and believe computer animation leads to a dead end.

Jar Jar Binks

However, these responses have not alleviated the worries of highly paid movie stars who are concerned not only about the emergence of digital competition, but also about how their images could be used in photo-real computer animation. They fear that this technology may allow unscrupulous moviemakers to use actors' images without their knowledge or consent.

Photo-real computer technology is regularly used to insert actors into film clips with historical figures and to resurrect long-dead stars such as John Wayne or Humphrey Bogart for use in commercials. In addition, actors worry that directors will alter or augment their performance, with or without their permission. This technique is used routinely when a script calls for actors to grow older in a film. A digital image of the actor is taken, signs of aging are digitally removed, and youthful features are added.

If animation technology and artistry continue to improve, it will be possible for directors to reach deep into a filmed performance and change more than laugh lines or crow's feet. An actor's performance could be completely altered on screen by technicians, giving the actor no control over his or her craft. And if many filmmakers have their way, virtual actors cannot be far behind.

3 Answer the questions. Compare your answers with a partner's.

a. Why were actors difficult to digitalize until now?

b. What is the reaction of real actors to the digital characters?

c. What are the advantages of digital actors?

d. What is the main concern of people who oppose the idea of digital actors?

e. Besides creating digital actors, what are some other applications of the technological tools described in the article?

Write the letter of the key ideas below next to the paragraph in the reading where it appeared.

   a. The idea of using virtual actors is popular with producers.

   b. Actors do not feel their performances can be replicated by digital characters.

   c. The main concern of actors is that their image may be used improperly.

   d. Filmmakers already use technology to alter actors' performances.

 Vocabulary Check Match the words from the reading on the left with their meanings on the right.

_____ **1.** whimper (line 16)	**a.** lines around the eyes
_____ **2.** dead end (line 35)	**b.** bring back to life
_____ **3.** alleviate (line 36)	**c.** give a soft cry of pain or sadness
_____ **4.** emergence (line 38)	**d.** wide expanse or scope
_____ **5.** unscrupulous (line 41)	**e.** act of appearing
_____ **6.** resurrect (line 43)	**f.** add to; improve
_____ **7.** augment (line 45)	**g.** make something less severe
_____ **8.** crow's feet (line 51)	**h.** a street or path that is closed at one end
	i. without moral principles

Think About It

 Is the actors' fear that their image might be misused justified? Aside from actors, who else might be a target of this technology?

 How can actors and celebrities protect their images from being digitally misused?

Write: The Analytical Essay

The analytical essay examines an issue or problem, breaks it down into parts, and looks at each part closely. Its purpose may be to provide an overview of a subject, to present a particular point of view, or to compare and contrast.

 A Persuasive Essay A persuasive essay presents and develops an opinion. It contains a thesis statement stating an opinion and arguments and supporting evidence for the opinion. If arguments against the opinion appear, then so does evidence to refute those arguments.

8 As you read the essay write the appropriate letter next to the corresponding section of the text. Letters can be used more than once.

a. introduction
b. thesis statement
c. argument for the opinion

d. argument against the opinion
e. supporting evidence
f. summarizing statement

Technology AND THE Future OF Film

Until recently, moviemaking was regarded as accessible to only a select few. Now, all this is changing with the emergence of newly-developed digital technologies. These technologies, such as the digital video (DV) camcorder and editing software for home computers, have the potential to revolutionize the movie industry by placing the means of artistic production in more hands then ever before. But will this change the essence of filmmaking? The creative process is more than the sum of the technologies involved, and it is not at all clear that the digital revolution will have as great an impact on the movie industry as it has had on some other industries.

Many film critics, filmmakers, and industry insiders have suggested that the digital era will open the world to a new generation of artists with no previous access to or experience in the movie business. A massive number of camera-less screenwriters will have the opportunity to express their brand-new ideas. Industry insiders maintain that this accessibility will ease the process of filmmaking and make it as inexpensive as writing.

A second point is that digital technology will open new markets for an emerging generation of non-professional films. Because of the availability and portability of the new equipment, they claim more films will be produced by unknowns than ever before. However, will there be audiences for this flood of new films? Brilliant movies have disappeared after being shown at a film festival, and this had nothing to do with the film; it had to do with audience demand and distribution problems.

In conclusion, the new technologies clearly have great potential. Nevertheless, they will not be a substitute for talent. Perhaps one day we will develop tools that will help the creative process and overcome the problems of distribution. For the time being, though, we are left to wait for the next revolution in filmmaking.

Write About It

9 Write a brief essay on the effects of violent films on society.

   10 **Check Your Writing** Exchange papers with a partner. Use the questions below to give feedback to your partner. When you get your paper back, revise as necessary.

- Is there a clear thesis statement?
- Do all the body paragraphs support the thesis statement?
- Does each paragraph have a topic sentence?
- Do the details in each paragraph support the topic sentence?

GRAMMAR

A Circle the letter of the correct answer to complete each sentence.

1. One of the most significant first-time events of my life was when   A ⒷC D
    I _____ my first car.
    (A) buy   **(C)** am buying
    (B) bought   **(D)** have bought

2. The car _____ old and used, but that didn't matter at all.   A B C D
    (A) is   **(C)** was
    (B) isn't   **(D)** weren't

3. All I cared about was that, finally, I _____ a set of wheels.   A B C D
    (A) am getting   **(C)** had gotten
    (B) were getting   **(D)** have gotten

4. Even today, almost forty years later, when I close my eyes,   A B C D
    I _____ it parked in my driveway.
    (A) saw   **(C)** have seen
    (B) see   **(D)** am seeing

5. I remember the day I _____ it a beautiful red with black   A B C D
    racing stripes.
    (A) had painted   **(C)** paint
    (B) have painted   **(D)** painted

6. I can almost _____ my fingers touching the sleek,   A B C D
    leather-covered steering wheel, still today.
    (A) feel   **(C)** be feeling
    (B) felt   **(D)** was feeling

7. I loved that car, and the crazy thing is that I really _____   A B C D
    that car loved me.
    (A) believe   **(C)** have believed
    (B) believed   **(D)** am believing

8. I guess a person just never _____ her first car.   A B C D
    (A) has forgotten   **(C)** forgot
    (B) had forgotten   **(D)** forgets

ANSWERING ERROR DETECTION QUESTIONS Some standardized tests present questions to determine if you are able to identify grammar mistakes. In some tests, students are also asked to correct the mistakes. Before answering, read each answer choice. While these tasks focus on verbs you learned in Units 1-3, most error detection tasks test all types of grammar.

B Each sentence has four underlined words or phrases. One of these underlined words or phrases is incorrect. Circle the letter of the word or phrase that is incorrect.

SECTION ONE

1. Many people <u>predict</u> that our relationships with food <u>is changing</u>   A (B) C D
                         A   B
    as we <u>learn</u> <u>to make</u> better food choices.
              C   D

2. There<u>'s</u> a lecture about this tomorrow morning, but unfortunately,   A B C D
            A
    I <u>can't</u> <u>be going</u> because <u>I'm taking</u> an exam for another class
         B   C   D
    at that time.

3. Although my exam <u>starts</u> at 8:00, and the lecture <u>doesn't start</u> until   A B C D
                              A   B
    9:00, I think it <u>is taking</u> me more than an hour <u>to finish</u> the exam.
                          C   D

4. I know the exam <u>is going to be</u> very difficult even though <u>I've been study</u>   A B C D
                            A   B
    for it for the last five days, because all the other tests <u>we've taken</u> for
                                                                      C
    that class <u>have been</u> difficult.
                    D

5. However, I strongly recommend you <u>attend</u> the lecture because there   A B C D
                                                A
    <u>aren't</u> any more lectures on this topic scheduled, and <u>I believe</u> this one
       B   C
    <u>is being</u> particularly interesting.
       D

SECTION TWO

1. The story <u>is</u> that Isaac Newton <u>was sitting</u> under an apple tree when   A B C D
                   A   B
    an apple <u>was falling</u> from a tree and <u>hit</u> him on his head.
                  C   D

2. People <u>have believed</u> that Newton <u>hadn't thought</u> about the force of   A B C D
           A   **B**

   gravity before the apple <u>fell</u> on his head and <u>gave</u> him the idea.
                        C   **D**

3. However, it <u>is</u> more likely that Newton <u>has wondered</u> about gravity   A B C D
              A   **B**

   for a long time before the apple <u>fell</u>, but that the falling apple <u>helped</u>
                                C   **D**

   to clarify his thoughts.

VOCABULARY

A Circle the letter of the word(s) that comes closest in meaning to the **boldface** word(s) in each sentence.

SECTION ONE

1. Many famous scientists end up discovering things they had never   A (B) C D
   set out to discover.
   (A) needed   (C) wanted
   (B) intended   (D) hoped

2. The digital images of the future will be **pristine** compared   A B C D
   to the images movie audiences see today.
   (A) fantastic   (C) creative
   (B) unspoiled   (D) technological

3. There have been a multitude of **start-up** digital graphics and   A B C D
   animation companies in the last few years.
   (A) heavy-duty   (C) worn-out
   (B) newly-created   (D) fast-lane

4. People wonder if the **emergence** of new technologies in virtual   A B C D
   reality will make it more difficult to identify what is real and
   what is virtual.
   (A) success   (C) profitability
   (B) creativity   (D) appearance

5. Movies, whether or not they are the type currently being made or the type that will be made in the future, can make **tall tales** seem believable.

    (A) complicated stories   **(C)** strange stories

    (B) long-lasting stories   **(D)** untrue stories

A B C D

6. There is a huge difference between being **adept** and being truly creative when it comes to the art of movie making.

    (A) skillful   **(C)** expressive

    (B) trained   **(D)** knowledgeable

A B C D

SECTION TWO

1. Scientists claim that the latest technology in earthquake prediction can provide people with a warning of an **impending** earthquake.

    (A) approaching   **(C)** powerful

    (B) unexpected   **(D)** dangerous

A B C D

2. Some of the most successful new products have names that are short and **catchy**.

    (A) smart-sounding   **(C)** nicelooking

    (B) attention-getting   **(D)** easygoing

A B C D

3. My film professor advised us to **alleviate** the pain of rejection by working harder.

    (A) identify   **(C)** explore

    (B) highlight   **(D)** reduce

A B C D

4. Being **congenial** can help you get a part in the film industry.

    (A) moody   **(C)** friendly

    (B) sleepy   **(D)** lazy

A B C D

GETTING STARTED

Warm Up

1 Learning how to deal with conflicts productively is an important social skill. What is your definition of conflict? Work in small groups. Brainstorm common situations in which conflict occurs.

2 Think of a situation in which you disagreed or "begged to differ" with a relative, friend, classmate, or boss. What was the disagreement about? How did you eventually resolve the problem?

3 Listen to three arguments. Write the subject of each dispute on the lines. How would you resolve each one?

a. _____

_____

b. _____

_____

c. _____

_____

Figure It Out

People have different ways of handling conflict. What are yours? Check the statements on the questionnaire on page 44 that tell how well you deal with disagreement.

Dealing with Disagreement

How do you usually behave?

_____ 1. I avoid getting into quarrels by leaving the scene.

_____ 2. In disagreements, I never try to disguise my true feelings.

_____ 3. When someone disagrees with me, I work hard at convincing the other person to accept my way of thinking.

_____ 4. I try to take responsibility for my thoughts and feelings by saying "I feel hurt . . . ." rather than "You hurt me . . . ."

_____ 5. When I have a dispute with someone, I sometimes refuse to discuss the situation. I feel that talking about it will only make things worse.

_____ 6. I work hard at empathizing with the other person so I can see the situation in the same way that the other person does.

_____ 7. I need to establish who is to blame before I can even think about resolving the problem.

_____ 8. I always try to validate other people's feelings; I let them know I think their feelings are reasonable.

_____ 9. I can't help bringing up old grievances during arguments.

_____ 10. I try to emphasize those things we agree on before discussing anything we might disagree on.

_____ 11. When I'm upset, it's difficult for me to consider the other person's viewpoint. I find myself doing most of the talking.

_____ 12. I'm cautious about expressing my opinions; I don't state them emphatically.

_____ 13. I try to avoid saying "no" directly.

_____ 14. Being willing to change my opinion is important to me.

How many odd-numbered items did you check?_____

How many even-numbered items did you check?_____

According to experts, you are following recommended conflict resolution strategies if you checked mostly even-numbered statements.

4 Work with a partner. Take turns guessing what each other's answers to the questions were. Then compare your guesses with your partner's answers.

5 **Vocabulary Check** Match the words on the left with their meanings on the right.

_____ 1. disguise   **a.** unable to change or stop doing something

_____ 2. empathizing   **b.** learn whether something is true or not

_____ 3. validate   **c.** complaint

_____ 4. can't help   **d.** hide, cover up

_____ 5. grievance   **e.** putting yourself in someone else's position

                    f. discovering

Talk About It

6 An angry office worker is telling a sympathetic listener about a problem she has with their boss. Work with a partner. Take turns being the worker and the listener, and discuss the accusations below. Use the conversation as a model.

Example: you aren't working hard enough

ROLES	MODEL CONVERSATION	FUNCTIONS
Worker:	I'm so mad! Our boss just accused me of being unfocused and not getting things done on time!	Talk about a conflict.
Listener:	Oh, I'm sorry to hear that. What happened exactly?	Empathize and ask for more information.
Worker:	Well, she actually had a point — I missed two very important deadlines, but it's only because I'm totally swamped. It's terrible!	Explain the circumstances.
Listener:	You need to tell our boss so she can find someone to help take some of the work off your shoulders.	Give advice.
Worker:	You're right. I will. Thanks for listening!	Agree or disagree. Express gratitude.

Accusations

    a. You're making too many personal phones calls at work.
    b. You arrive late every day.
    c. You're taking too many sick days.
    d. You're taking home office supplies.
    e. You're using your computer to surf the Internet instead of do work.
    f. (your own idea)

Gerunds

Gerunds are –*ing* forms of verbs used as nouns. They are used as subjects of sentences, objects of verbs, or objects of prepositions. They can also be used in the negative.

- **Yelling** will not make you right. (subject)
- You're a grown-up. You should stop **blaming** your parents for your problems. (object)
- I believe in **compromising**. (object of preposition)
- **Not responding** to her accusations was really hard, but it paid off. We get along great now. (negative gerund)

1 Find examples of each statement below in the questionnaire, and write them below the sentences. Compare your answers with a partner's.

a. A gerund is the -*ing* form of the verb used as a noun.

_____

b. A gerund can be the subject of a sentence.

_____

c. A gerund can be the object of the verb in the sentence.

_____

d. A gerund can follow a preposition.

_____

Verbs with Gerunds or Infinitives

Some verbs are usually followed by a gerund or an infinitive. Sometimes these verbs can be followed by an object before the gerund or infinitive.

Verbs Used with Gerunds
start/begin/continue/keep on/can't help/resume doing something
stop/finish/quit/resist doing something
avoid/delay/put off/resist/give up doing something
acknowledge/consider/risk doing something
appreciate/enjoy/feel like/dislike/miss doing something

Verbs Used with Infinitives

agree to stop	want to do	seem to like
afford to travel	manage to pass	refuse to go
decide to go	offer to help	volunteer to stop
expect to win	hope to talk	fail to succeed

Verbs Taking Objects Used with Infinitive

advise someone to study	permit someone to see
convince someone to go	persuade someone to buy
encourage someone to ask	remind someone to call
expect someone to pay	require someone to stay

Gerunds or Infinitives and Their Meanings

Some verbs can be followed by either the gerund or the infinitive with only a slight change in meaning. We use the gerund to convey a real, clear, or fulfilled action. We use the infinitive to convey a future or unfulfilled action.

Verb + Gerund or Infinitive

begin doing/to do	continue doing/to do	like doing/to do	prefer to do/doing
can't stand doing/to do	hate doing/to do	love doing/to do	start doing/to do

2 Ana and Jo are not happy with one another. A friend advised them to make a list of all the things that upset them. Complete the lists below with the correct form of the verbs from the box.

go out	do	be	listen	go	help	be	wear	try	take

ANA'S LIST:

- Jo always agrees (1.) _____ things with me but cancels at the last moment.
- She criticizes me for (2.) _____ bright clothes.
- Jo always avoids (3.) _____ with me and my other friends.
- Jo often blames me for (4.) _____ late even if she knows that I can't help it.
- She offered (5.) _____ me move but then cancelled at the last moment.

JO'S LIST:

- Ana refuses (6.) _____ to my CDs, and that hurts my feelings.
- Ana dislikes (7.) _____ shopping with me.
- She stopped me from (8.) _____ a belly dancing class even though I really wanted to.
- Every time I sleep late, she accuses me of (9.) _____ lazy.
- Ana always gives up (10.) _____ when things are too difficult. It makes me so mad!

With some verbs the meaning of the sentence changes if the verb is followed by a gerund or by an infinitive.

Verbs Used with Infinitive or Gerund (Change in Meaning)

Sue **stopped to smoke**. (Sue stopped in order to smoke. = She's a smoker.)

Sue **stopped smoking**. (Sue stopped the act of smoking. = She's no longer a smoker.)

I'll **remember to send** the package. (I won't forget.)

I'll **remember sending** the package. (I'll remember the act of sending the package.)

I **regret to inform** you. (I haven't informed you yet, I'm doing it now.)

I **regret informing**. (I regret the act of informing you. = It has been done.)

---

3 Match the underlined phrases with their meanings below. Write the number on the line.

___1___ **a.** **MOTHER:** Peter, you came home after midnight again last night. You should always <u>remember to call</u> us if you are going to be late.

___2___ **b.** **SON:** But I did. I distinctly <u>remember calling</u> you, but nobody picked up.
1. remember to perform a duty, responsibility, or task
2. remember something that happened before now

_____ **c.** **FRANCES:** I <u>regret to tell</u> you that I lost your coat.

_____ **d.** **MARIA:** I <u>regret telling</u> you that you could use my coat.
3. I haven't told you about losing it.
4. I already told you to use it.

_____ **e.** **PENNY:** I'm sorry I'm late, Mira, but I <u>stopped to buy</u> this great sweater on sale.

_____ **f.** **MIRA:** You have to <u>stop buying</u> so many clothes. You'll be broke soon.
5. pause in order to do something else
6. halt an action

4 Work with a partner. Take turns making short conversations for each situation. Use the appropriate form of the verbs in parentheses.

a. You are at the doctor's for your regular checkup. The doctor feels that there are many changes you have to make in your exercise and eating habits. (*stop*)

b. You have just found out that one of your students did not pass his final exam. You call him to tell him about it. (*regret*)

c. You are telling a friend some of the things you did as a kid. (*remember*)

d. You are telling your friend what you did on your way to her place. (*stop*)

Using *It* + Infinitive Instead of a Gerund

To make a general statement, we can begin sentences with a gerund or use *It's* + adjective + infinitive as the subject of the sentence.

> **Resolving** problems in a collaborative manner is an essential skill.
>
> MEANS
>
> **It's** essential **to resolve** problems in a collaborative manner.
>
> OR
>
> **It's** essential **for** employees **to resolve** problems in a collaborative manner.

  5 **Check Your Understanding** Complete the passage with the appropriate form of the verbs in parentheses.

Different cultures have various views on time, which result in different expectations about behavior. Different orientations toward time may lead to disagreements and conflicts in various situations. Some anthropologists recommend (**1. make a distinction**) _____ between two ways of viewing time: monochronic and polychronic. American culture is monochronic. (**2. treat**) _____ time as money and as something a person shouldn't waste is typical of monochronic cultures such as American culture. In monochronic cultures, people expect (**3. not, be**) _____ interrupted when doing things. On the other hand, people in polychronic cultures, such as Mexicans, generally enjoy (**4. do**) _____ many things at once. It is permitted and even expected (**5. interrupt**) _____ others. People also frequently stop (**6. do**) _____ a task before finishing it and beginning another one. Not surprisingly, people from monochronic and polychronic cultures may have problems because of their attitudes toward time. It is important to remember (**7. find out**) _____ as much as possible about the cultures of others when you are in a multicultural setting.

  6 **Express Yourself** Work with a partner. Write a dialogue for one of the conflicts mentioned in the passage above, and perform your dialogue for another pair.

LISTENING and SPEAKING

Listen: Resolving Conflict

1 **Before You Listen** Decide if you **A** (agree) or **D** (disagree) with the statements below. Then discuss your opinions in small groups.

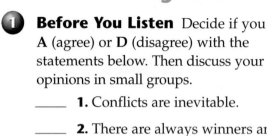

_____ **1.** Conflicts are inevitable.

_____ **2.** There are always winners and losers in any dispute.

_____ **3.** Communication makes a disagreement easier to resolve.

_____ **4.** It's important for parents to teach their children that "good children don't fight."

_____ **5.** It's important for parents to teach their children not to let a bully push them around.

STRATEGY **Applying Background Knowledge** When listening critically, effective listeners relate new information to background knowledge in order to assess the strengths and weaknesses of the speaker's point of view. They may also try to empathize, or put themselves in the position of the speaker.

2 Listen to a lecture about conflict resolution. Take notes, answer the questions, and compare your answers with a partner's.

a. What are the five styles the speaker mentions for dealing with conflict?

b. What are characteristics of each style?

3 Listen again and discuss the questions with a partner.

a. Based on your own experience, how beneficial is the speaker's lecture for you?

b. What are two examples from the lecture which you can relate to your own conflict resolution behavior?

Pronunciation

Contrastive Stress

Where we place stress in a sentence depends on several factors. When we want to signal contrast between two items in a sentence, we emphasize them both.

A: Is this a _competitive_ or _collaborative_ resolution strategy?

B: It's clearly a _collaborative_ strategy, not a _competitive_ one.

4 Work with a partner. Predict which words will be stressed in the following dialogue and underline them.

A: Is our conflict resolution class on Tuesday or Thursday?

B: Thursday, I think.

A: And do you remember the room? Is it 204 or 206?

B: Not sure about that. You should check the schedule.

A: OK. Will do that. And I'll see you tonight, right? Or is it tomorrow night?

B: You can't remember a single thing these days! It's tomorrow night. I'm busy tonight. I have a date with Steve, remember?

5 Listen to the dialogue to check your predictions.

6 Work with a partner. Practice reading the dialogues, focusing on contrastive stress.

Speak Out

 Managing Conflict Conflict can arise in discussions. To avoid misunderstanding, you should state your feelings and reactions as clearly as possible. You can express strong reactions politely by using softeners. These softeners allow you to politely communicate your feelings while maintaining a positive atmosphere.

7 Decide if the items state **P** (polite disagreement) or **I** (impolite disagreement).

_____ **1.** I'm sorry, but I'm very upset by this because I feel . . .

_____ **2.** You've got to be out of your mind to say that.

_____ **3.** To a certain extent I agree with you, but . . .

_____ **4.** I'm afraid I really don't agree with that because . . .

_____ **5.** That's ridiculous.

_____ **6.** OK, I see your point; however . . .

_____ **7.** You're completely off-base.

_____ **8.** I'm sorry, but that's not how I see it.

8 Work with a partner. Brainstorm reasons and examples to support each side of the conflict below. Then work in small groups with students acting as representatives for each side. Discuss the situation and decide how to resolve it. Use softeners in your discussion, and try to use a win/win approach to resolving the issue.

> **SITUATION**
>
> In the next academic year, all students will be required to buy personal computers, and all assignments must be done on computers. The students claim they cannot afford to buy the computers themselves. They insist that if the policy requires computers, it's the administration's duty to buy them. The administrators, on the other hand, feel that computers are class materials like textbooks. Students have to purchase their other class materials, so the administrators feel that buying computers is the responsibility of the students. The administrators and students are meeting to discuss the issue.

READING and WRITING

Read About It

 Before You Read Work with a partner. Discuss how you would react in the following situations.

    a. Your teacher criticizes you in front of the class.

    b. Your brand-new computer keeps crashing.

 Evaluating Points of View When reading for critical analysis, effective readers note the examples that a writer uses to support his or her argument. Then they draw on their own experience and knowledge to assess the credibility of those arguments and to evaluate the strengths and weaknesses of the author's point of view.

 Read the selection. As you read, note examples that the authors use to support their conclusions. How do their examples compare with your own experiences?

Say What You Mean
by Paulette Dale and James C. Wolf

Misunderstandings happen to everyone. They occur between friends, co-workers, and family members. Communication breakdowns can be as harmless as showing up for an appointment 5 half an hour early or as inconvenient as waiting in the rain for two hours for someone who never shows up. They can be as devastating as a failed relationship or a divorce. They can even be a matter of life and death. For example, 10 failure to communicate fuel shortages and other mechanical problems has been at the root of several airline disasters.

Miscommunication often occurs because either listeners do not pay attention carefully, or 15 they take for granted that they understand what a speaker means, when in fact, the speaker had intended a completely different meaning from what was understood. This was certainly the case with a shy college student named 20 Susanna who completely misinterpreted a comment from one of her professors.

Susanna felt self-conscious asking her professors questions in lecture halls that were filled with students. She finally summoned the 25 courage to ask her psychology professor a question. Before answering her, he replied, "That's an unusual query." Susanna felt insulted because she interpreted his remark to mean

her question was foolish. She was mortified. 30 She told the story to another teacher in tears. Her teacher was sure there had been a misunderstanding and encouraged her to approach her professor after class and ask him what he had really meant. Once she did so, 35 Susanna was surprised and relieved to find that her psychology professor had thought her question was unusually insightful. He had intended to compliment her, but she had taken his comment the wrong way.

40 Sometimes, when listeners misinterpret what has been said, they blame the speaker for being the source of the problem without asking the speaker for clarification. A lot of misunderstandings can be avoided by 45 determining what certain words mean before criticizing the speaker or the message. It's important to say to oneself, "I don't get it. I had better ask some questions because this might mean something else to another person."

50 Another source of miscommunication can come from differences between people's communication styles. Do they communicate their feelings and intentions directly or indirectly? Many individuals are reluctant to 55 state their feelings clearly and directly. They have a tendency to hint at what they want, or

"beat around the bush," by phrasing their needs and wants as questions rather than as statements. Communicating in this manner 60 can be very frustrating and confusing for people who are used to discussing things openly and assertively, saying exactly what they mean.

Although individuals within a culture differ, 65 communication styles exist within each culture. Differences between cultural communication styles can lead to "cross-cultural miscommunication." People from countries such as Turkey, the United States, Canada, 70 Australia, France, Germany, and Switzerland tend to have a direct communication style. They value assertiveness and like to say what they are thinking so that others know exactly how they feel about things. People from 75 countries such as Japan, Thailand, Korea, China, Peru, and Mexico tend to communicate relatively indirectly. In order to maintain harmony and avoid conflict, they rarely express disagreement in public for fear that 80 might make someone lose face.

If, for example, a person bought an item that turned out to be defective, his or her reaction would probably be influenced by his or her culture. A person from a culture with a 85 direct communication style would probably return it to the store. He or she might say, "This product is defective. I would like a refund, please." If refused, that person might ask to see the manager and repeat the 90 request. On the other hand, a person from a culture with a more indirect style might not even return the item to the store. If he or she did, then this person might apologize to the salesclerk for being a bother before asking for 95 an exchange or a refund. Alternatively, the person might show it to the salesclerk and ask, "Could you do something about this?" in the hope of being offered an exchange or a refund without directly asking for one. If the 100 request were denied, it's likely that this person would leave the store without pursuing the matter further but never shop there again.

Thanks to advances in global travel and communications, the world has 105 become a smaller place. In the future, you will very likely be communicating more and more with people from different cultures. Appreciating and valuing cultural differences, including those behind 110 communication styles, helps to promote understanding and successful interaction among people from diverse backgrounds.

 Discuss these questions in small groups.

a. According to the authors, what are the most common causes of miscommunication?

b. How did Susanna's teacher advise her to deal with her psychology professor? Would that same advice work with the professors you've worked with? Why or why not?

c. In your opinion, which communication style do the authors prefer? Why do you think so? What style of communication do you think is favored in the authors' culture? Why?

  Vocabulary Check Match the words on the left with their meanings on the right.

_____ **1.** at the root of (line 11)
_____ **2.** take for granted (line 15)
_____ **3.** insightful (line 37)
_____ **4.** take it the wrong way (line 39)
_____ **5.** get it (line 47)
_____ **6.** beat around the bush (line 57)
_____ **7.** lose face (line 80)

a. misinterpret something
b. damage personal prestige
c. not come to the point
d. understanding something
e. harmful
f. the cause of
g. understanding
h. assume

Think About It

 In general, what is the communication style of your country? What advice would you give to visitors about communicating in your country?

Write: Choosing and Narrowing a Topic

An analytical essay examines an issue or problem to present a point of view, compare and contrast, or persuade. Whatever its purpose, it is important that you choose a topic that is appropriately narrow and specific.

© The New Yorker Collection, 2001. Jack Ziegler from cartoonbank.com. All Rights Reserved.

STRATEGY Effective writers choose their topics carefully. If the topic is too broad, there will be too much information to deal with. If it is too narrow, there will not be enough information to use. Therefore, the topic should be narrow and specific. Begin by first selecting a broad topic that interests you. Then narrow your topic to something more specific.

If you want to write a paper about the topic *conflict resolution*, you will find that there is too much information for a single paper. And if you narrow the topic to *conflict resolution among Colombian coffee farmers in January 1980*, the topic is too narrow, and you won't have enough information. However, if your topic is *conflict resolution among Colombian coffee farmers*, your topic is both appropriately narrow and suitably specific.

Write About It

 Choose a topic related to conflict resolution and write a short analytical composition about it. Before you begin, make sure your topic is narrow and specific, and decide on the purpose of your paper. Be sure to include a thesis statement as well as information and support for the main idea.

  Check Your Writing Exchange papers with a partner. Use the questions to give feedback to your partner. When you get your own paper back, revise as necessary.

- Is the topic appropriately narrow and specific?
- Is there a clear thesis statement?
- Do the information and details support the thesis statement?
- What is the purpose of the paper?

ODD JOBS

GETTING STARTED

Warm Up

When you ask people what they do for a living, most will give you answers you recognize: doctor, teacher, or sales clerk. But some people have more unusual jobs: puppeteer, advice columnist, or statue cleaner.

1 Work with a partner. Brainstorm a list of unusual jobs and share your list with the class.

 2 Listen to three people talk about their jobs. What does each do for a living?

Figure It Out

Terry is telling his friend Hank all about his new job.

>**HANK:** Hey, Terry. I hear you have a new job!
>
>**TERRY:** Yes, my tax accounting days are over. I'm a skydive videographer now.
>
>**HANK:** Skydive what?
>
>**TERRY:** Skydive videographer. I videotape people doing skydives. I make
>5   a video story of their day. These videos are mementos of really unique experiences.
>
>**HANK:** What a job! What ever made you get started doing something like that? What a daredevil you turned out to be.
>
>**TERRY:** I got hooked when I made my first skydive. I just loved the sensation
>10   of freefall. Now I have 2,700 skydives under my belt, and 1,800 of them are video jumps.

HANK: Wow! Video jumps! Where do you keep the camera during the filming? You hold it in your hands?

TERRY: Well, not exactly. My two cameras are attached to my helmet.

15 HANK: So, how does one of those cameras work?

TERRY: It's automatic. A switch has to be pressed for it to start filming, and I have that switch close to my hand.

HANK: And what happens during the skydive?

TERRY: I exit the aircraft with the person jumping and film the freefall. I land 20 and I film the client's landing. The footage is then edited into a professionally designed video.

HANK: It's amazing that you actually do this for a living!

TERRY: It's a tad unusual, but I get to do something I love. Here's our brochure.

HANK: Thanks, I'll take a look. But I have to tell you, Terry, when I tried 25 skydiving, I got so scared I backed out at the last moment—literally! I'm just happy my cowardice wasn't videotaped.

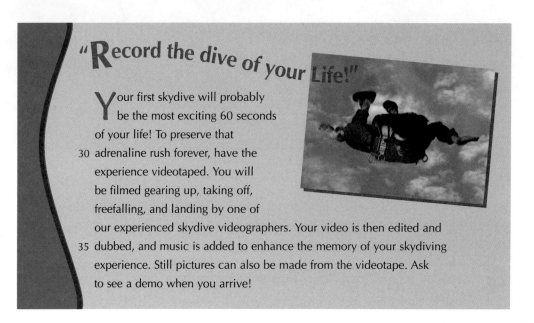

"Record the dive of your Life!"

Your first skydive will probably be the most exciting 60 seconds of your life! To preserve that 30 adrenaline rush forever, have the experience videotaped. You will be filmed gearing up, taking off, freefalling, and landing by one of our experienced skydive videographers. Your video is then edited and 35 dubbed, and music is added to enhance the memory of your skydiving experience. Still pictures can also be made from the videotape. Ask to see a demo when you arrive!

 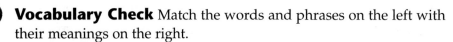 **Vocabulary Check** Match the words and phrases on the left with their meanings on the right.

_____ **1.** daredevil (line 8)   **a.** become addicted to

_____ **2.** get hooked (line 9)   **b.** be experienced in something

_____ **3.** to have under one's belt (line 10)   **c.** lack of courage

_____ **4.** back out (line 25)   **d.** equipment

_____ **5.** cowardice (line 26)   **e.** someone who takes a lot of risks

_____ **6.** gear up (line 32)   **f.** withdraw, cancel

                                        g. get necessary equipment ready

Talk About It

 4 Alicia and Daniel have just met in a ceramics class and are discussing Alicia's job. Work with a partner. Take turns discussing the different jobs below. Use the conversation as a model.

Example: Perfume tester

ROLES	MODEL CONVERSATION	FUNCTIONS
Daniel:	So, tell me, what do you do for a living?	Ask about a job.
Alicia:	I'm a perfume tester.	Name the job.
Daniel:	A perfume tester! Wow—now that's a job! So how did you become a perfume tester? Is any previous experience required?	Express surprise and ask for details.
Alicia:	No, not really. You're trained before you start working. But a keen sense of smell is considered a real plus.	Explain the job.
Daniel:	And what do you like best about the job?	Ask for more information.
Alicia:	Well, I'd have to say it's all the free samples I get. I have a great collection of perfume.	Elaborate.

Jobs

a. restaurant critic

b. wedding planner

c. house sitter

d. juggler

e. psychic

f. (your own idea)

GRAMMAR

The Passive Voice: Past and Present

Passive and active sentences often have similar meanings, but the focus is different. We use the passive to focus on the process or action. We use the passive when the agent (who is doing the action) is unknown, generally understood, or not important. Usually the agent is not expressed unless it is considered important. It is introduced with the preposition *by*.

	Passive Voice (focus on the process or action)
Simple present	George Zambelli **is considered** the King of Fireworks.
Present progressive	Fireworks **are** still **being produced** by the Zambelli family.
Present perfect	More than 25 percent of fireworks used in the United States **have been produced** by descendants of Italian immigrants.
Simple past	The Zambelli fireworks recipes **were written down** in a little black book by family members and **carried** across the Atlantic at the beginning of the 20th century.
Past progressive	Firework explosive chemicals **were being packed** into a small tube when I visited the Zambelli Fireworks factory.
Past perfect	By the end of the 20th century, thousands of tons of fireworks **had** already **been produced** by the Zambelli Fireworks Company.

1 Read the passage and answer the questions that follow.

How would you like to do the things you love best—shopping, dining, watching movies—and get paid for them? If you're looking for a part-time job that is easy and fun to do—well, you've definitely <u>come</u> to the right place! We can offer you a job as a mystery shopper: you'll be a customer in disguise, evaluating the quality of service employees of a certain store, restaurant, or hotel <u>give</u> to customers.

Here's the story of Rachel Gordon, a mystery shopper. With her shorts, T-shirt, and sweatshirt, she <u>looks</u> like any other mom out shopping. Today she's <u>going</u> undercover to check out a local store in a large grocery store chain. The store manager <u>has asked</u> her to do a general review of the store. Her review <u>begins</u> with a quick look at the glass doors to the store. No points gained here—the person responsible <u>hasn't washed</u> them in at least a week. Then she casually <u>enters</u> the store, walking from aisle to aisle and <u>noticing</u> everything from the neatly arranged racks with fruits and vegetables to the spilled rice on the floor. Finally, at the checkout, she notes how the cashier deals with the customers (friendly or unfriendly), and then uses a $100 bill to see if the cashier will examine it closely. After the trip, she <u>rushes</u> to her home office to write up her observations. Although the shopping trip <u>took</u> only about half an hour, her eight-to ten-page report will take her about three hours to complete.

> **HELP WANTED:**
> Mystery shoppers are needed in your area NOW.
> Go shopping, eat out, see a movie–and **GET PAID!**

1. Which of the underlined verbs can be changed to the passive?
   Example: The quality of service employees <u>give</u> to customers ➔ the quality of service given to customers by employees
2. Which of the underlined verbs cannot be changed to the passive?
   Example: you've definitely come ➔ passive is not possible
3. What kinds of verbs cannot be changed to the passive?
   a. stative verbs
   b. action verbs
   c. verbs which do not take direct objects
   d. verbs with direct objects
   e. verbs with indirect objects

The Passive Voice: Modal Verbs

The passive voice is also used with modals and similar expressions.

> **Passive Voice**
>
> The laws on fireworks safety **will be tightened** in the near future.
>
> Children **shouldn't be allowed** to play with fireworks.
>
> Natural fiber clothing **has to be worn** by fireworks makers because an explosion **could be caused** by a static electricity spark.

2 Complete the passage with the correct forms of the verbs. In some cases there may be more than one correct answer.

Mask making is a fascinating enterprise. With a few exceptions, masks (**1. make**) _____ by professionals who have many years of apprenticeship behind them. In societies where masks (**2. play**) _____ an important ceremonial role, it (**3. presume**) _____ that the spirit of the mask image (**4. feel**) _____ by the artist while creating the mask. Certain prescribed rituals (**5. follow**) _____ in the process of creating the mask. A spirit power (**6. believe**) _____ also to inhabit the artist's tools, so those (**7. handle**) _____ in a prescribed manner as well. If all the conventions (**8. adhere**) _____ to, the finished mask (**9. consider**) _____ to be filled with great supernatural power when it (**10. wear**) _____. Some cultures (**11. believe**) _____ that because of the close association between the mask maker and the spirit of the mask, some of the magic power (**12. absorb**) _____ by the mask maker.

MondoNovo Maschere by Guerrino Lovato

☑ ③ **Check Your Understanding** Check the situations in which you are most likely to use the passive form.

◻ **a.** Describing the steps in developing film
◻ **b.** Describing someone's work history
◻ **c.** A fortune teller describing a client's future
◻ **d.** Reporting on the production of olive oil

④ **Express Yourself** Work with a partner. What would your dream job be? Imagine the most interesting and unusual job you could have. Think about the job in detail, and discuss it with your partner.

LISTENING and SPEAKING

Listen: Storm Chasers

① **Before You Listen** Have you ever heard of storm chasers? What kinds of people do you think they are, and why do they chase storms? Have you ever done anything similar?

STRATEGY **Recognizing Categories** Effective listeners use several strategies when listening for understanding. One of these is listening for categories. Categorizing information helps listeners to organize information, especially those characteristics that distinguish items from each other. Good listeners also listen critically by using knowledge they already have to *infer* information that is not stated directly.

② Listen to a radio interview, and note the four categories of storm chasers mentioned. Include a description of each one.

③ Listen again. Decide if the sentences are **T** (true) or **F** (false). Compare your answers in groups.

_____ **a.** Mark Warren is not a city person.
_____ **b.** The least busy season for Mark Warren is summer.
_____ **c.** Mark doesn't approve of "yahoos."
_____ **d.** Mark is doing this kind of work for the money.
_____ **e.** Mark would enjoy skydiving and other extreme sports.

Pronunciation

> **Stress Patterns in Compound Nouns and Adjectives**
>
> Compound words, such as noun + noun and adjective + noun, have a regular stress pattern. Primary stress usually falls on the stressed syllable of the first word. The syllable of the second word that is usually stressed receives secondary stress.
>
> a báck-<u>bréak</u>ing jób
>
> Fóurth-of-Jú<u>ly</u> fíreworks by Zam<u>bélli</u>

4 Predict the stress pattern of the italicized words below. Put an accent mark (´) over the word with primary stress, and underline the syllables with secondary stress.

Laura Grant set out a tray of *mouthwatering* chocolate truffles as she sat down to talk to me about her job as a *chocolate taster*. She is one of the top *chocolate tasters* in *North America*, but her *master status* took years to attain. It feels like a *well-earned* Ph.D., she says! Laura doesn't use terms such as "dark" or "milk" to describe chocolate. Instead, her own *dessert classification system* includes: "amazingly good" for *high-grade* chocolate; "not amazing but good" for average chocolate, and "horrible" for a *poor-quality* chocolate made up of *cocoa powder*, sugar, and *vegetable oil*.

The day before she met with me, Laura had taken part in a *chocolate-tasting competition*. Together with other *blindfolded competitors*, she had to identify the name of the chocolate maker, the percentage of chocolate actually used, and the type of *chocolate bean* the chocolate came from. She finished as one of the *top five* competitors!

 5 Listen to the passage to check your predictions.

6 Work with a partner. Take turns reading the passage, focusing on the stress of the compound words.

Speak Out

STRATEGY **Maintaining Understanding in a Discussion** Misunderstandings occur when people assume that something is clear to everyone when it is not. In order to make sure that everyone in a discussion has the same understanding, it is important to request clarification of points when necessary and to be able to clarify your own ideas and explain those of others.

7 Decide if each expression is **A** (asking for clarification), **C** (clarifying ideas), or **P** (paraphrasing the ideas of someone else). Compare your answers with a partner's.

_____ **a.** Do you mean to say that…?

_____ **b.** In other words, he's saying that…

_____ **c.** Actually, that's not what I meant. What I wanted to say was…

_____ **d.** I'm not sure what you mean by that.

_____ **e.** I'm sorry, I'm not following you. Could you be more specific?

_____ **f.** So, what he really means is…

_____ **g.** Let me put it this way…

_____ **h.** If I understood you correctly, you're saying that…

_____ **i.** What I'm trying to say is…

_____ **j.** I think her point is that…

8 Work in small groups. Discuss the cartoons and explain how you would interpret the humor in each. Use the language above for clarifying and paraphrasing ideas.

THE FAR SIDE® BY GARY LARSON

"Well, hey… these things just snap right off."

The Far Side® by Gary Larson
©1983 FarWorks, Inc. All Rights Reserved.
Used with permission.

HERMAN®
by Jim Unger

8-11   © Jim Unger/dist. by United Media, 2001

"Harry, quick, get over here."

HERMAN® is reprinted with permission from
Laughingstock Licensing Inc., Ottawa, Canada.
All Rights Reserved.

READING and WRITING

Read About It

1 **Before You Read** Work with a partner. Brainstorm jobs which involve food. Share your ideas with the class.

STRATEGY **Using Graphic Organizers** When reading for understanding, efficient readers categorize information as they read. One way is to use a graphic organizer, such as a cluster or an idea map, to classify and organize ideas while reading. Look at the cluster below.

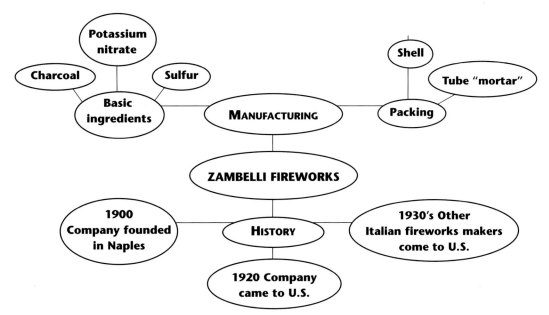

2 As you read the article, in the margin make a note of the main topics developed. Then share your ideas with a partner.

A Sweet Job

Imagine spending all day long tasting ice cream and getting paid for it! Sound too good to be true? Well, meet Carlo Buontalenti. He is the Chief Flavor Development Specialist for a top ice-cream company in the U.S. In addition to tasting ice cream, Buontalenti has sometimes used his well-honed taste buds to invent new ice-cream flavors, such as Cappuccino Mousse.

5 Ice cream is in his genes—his family has been in the ice-cream business for five generations, starting with his great-great-grandfather, who owned a *gelateria* (ice-cream parlor) in Italy in the 1850s. His family moved to the U.S. in the 1950s, where they opened up their own ice-cream store in keeping with the family tradition. The stores caught on, and a business was born. In his twenty-five years on the job, he estimates that he has made his way through at least 150

10 million gallons of ice cream.

Does this sound like a career you'd like to pursue? Well, it may be a sweet job, but it does carry some weighty responsibilities. One of the hardships Buontalenti faces is maintaining his

(continued on next page)

round physique. After all, who would trust a skinny ice-cream taster? Another is that he needs to make many sacrifices when it comes to food. Buontalenti has to eat a special diet to protect
15 his taste buds, which are insured for a million dollars. He avoids spicy foods and any food prepared with garlic or onion. He also avoids coffee, tea, and soda, since they taint his ability to taste the ice cream's delicate array of flavors. Finally, he has to pass on carbonated drinks and sodas, alcohol, tobacco, and even after-shave!

Buontalenti gets going every morning with a cup of herbal tea and then it's ice cream all day.
20 As he digs into carton after carton of ice cream, he resembles a methodical scientist conducting an experiment. His tools include a gold tasting-spoon and an instant-read thermometer. Unlike plastic or wood, gold leaves no aftertaste which might influence the flavor of the ice cream. The instant-read thermometer is used to gauge the temperature of the ice cream. He waits until it has attained the perfect temperature—forty-one degrees Fahrenheit, or five degrees Celsius, and then dives in.

25 Just like a wine taster, Buontalenti doesn't really eat the ice cream he tastes. He puts into practice the three S's: swirl, smack, and spit. During the tasting, the focus is not just on flavor, but also appearance and texture. Buontalenti's years of experience and razor-sharp buds
30 mean that even the smallest of problems can be detected when he checks the appearance, texture, bouquet, aroma, and taste of the ice cream. He rejects anything which is too coarse, crumbly, fluffy, or icy, or any cream which is starting to turn sour. His delicate
35 taste buds can even spot a hint of the bleach used to clean the ice-cream machines. A lack of sweetness or too much sweetness can be a problem as well.
As a result, the ice cream that does make it through this methodical process is appetizing in color and texture, has good body, and has a smooth and creamy flavor.

40 Interested in tasting ice cream like a professional? Here's what to do, according to the chief himself. The ice cream should be stored at twenty-three degrees Fahrenheit (five below zero Celsius) to maintain its freshness. When eaten, it should be set out until it reaches forty-one degrees F. To taste the ice cream like a professional, put the spoon upside down so it goes directly on your taste buds, then swirl it around, so it reaches all of the 9,000 taste buds in your mouth. Smack your
45 lips to allow air to reach the ice cream and ask yourself, "Is this ice cream smooth and creamy?" Once you've gotten the whole sensation, spit it out, and move on to the next sample.

It doesn't matter if Buontalenti is on a national tour to promote a new ice-cream flavor, in his kitchen experimenting with new flavors, or checking the quality of ice-cream, his main goal is always to campaign for top-quality ice cream. He advises ice-cream lovers to pack the
50 ice cream in a paper bag, not plastic, so it keeps colder, to stash it well back in the freezer, and to cover any left-over ice cream with a plastic wrap before putting the lid back on.

And what does the future hold for ice-cream lovers? To fit into today's health-conscious lifestyles, there'll be more vitamin-fortified ice creams and low-fat frozen yogurts, Buontalenti predicts. He also envisions this comfort food changing to fit into our rushed lifestyles and
55 envisions more sandwich-type ice creams and "mini-bites".

But no matter the flavor, size, shape, or color, ice cream will be ice cream, to be savored by many generations to come. Enjoy!

3 Work with a partner. Go back to the main topics you identified in Exercise 2. Decide on the three you find most interesting and put them in a cluster.

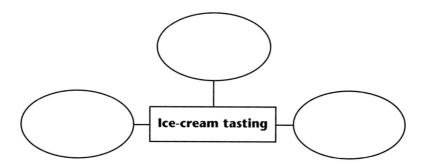

Ice-cream tasting

4 **Vocabulary Check** Match the words on the left with their meanings on the right. Compare your answers with a partner's.

_____ **1.** well-honed (line 4)   **a.** open and close your lips

_____ **2.** pursue (line 11)   **b.** go after, strive for

_____ **3.** hardship (line 12)   **c.** highly skilled

_____ **4.** taste buds (line 15)   **d.** taste and enjoy

_____ **5.** swirl (lines 27, 44)   **e.** without trouble

_____ **6.** smack (lines 27, 44)   **f.** move by twisting, turning

_____ **7.** stash (line 50)   **g.** have in mind, foresee

_____ **8.** envision (line 55)   **h.** keep, store

_____ **9.** savor (line 56)   **i.** difficulty

                                          j. cells on the tongue which sense
                                               sweetness, sourness, etc.

Think About It

5 How do you interpret the following saying: _"If you do what you like, you'll never work a day in your life?"_ Exchange ideas in small groups.

Write: Writing Introductions for Analytical Essays

Effective writers begin their essays with a paragraph that both engages the reader and gives the reader specific information about what to expect. A good introduction to an essay consists of three things: an attention-getting first sentence, a thesis statement, and a brief overview of how the essay will be organized—that is, what will be discussed first, second, and so on.

6 Read each introductory paragraph below. Note the topic, the writer's main point about the topic, and how you think the writer will develop the essay.

a. Working as a costumed movie character, such as Mickey Mouse, King Kong, or ET, is not fun and games. It can be hard work for several reasons. For one thing, you have to remain in character for long periods of time. Also, the costumes can be uncomfortable,

Unit 5

65

especially on a hot summer day. Furthermore, it can be difficult to perform normal functions, such as eating and sitting.

TOPIC: _____

MAIN POINT: _____

DEVELOPMENT: _____

b. Would you like to travel, live well, and meet new people? If your answer to any of these questions is yes, you might want to explore the possibilities of working on a cruise ship. Working on a cruise ship allows you to make money while taking a resort vacation. However, before you apply, you should consider whether or not you'd enjoy this type of lifestyle. What kind of person makes a good cruise ship employee? Here's a portrait of a typical cruise ship worker.

TOPIC: _____

MAIN POINT: _____

DEVELOPMENT: _____

Write About It

7 Look at the pictures of people doing "odd" jobs below. Choose a topic related to odd jobs. Decide what main point you want to make and what form of development would best support your main point in an essay. Write an introductory paragraph for an essay about that topic.

Circus Performer

Puppeteer

Chocolate Maker

8 Check Your Writing Exchange paragraphs with a partner. Use the questions below to give feedback to your partner. When you get your own paper back, revise as necessary.

- Is the topic clear and easy to identify?
- Does the topic engage the reader?
- What main points will be covered in the essay?
- How will the essay be developed?

BEHOLDING BEAUTY

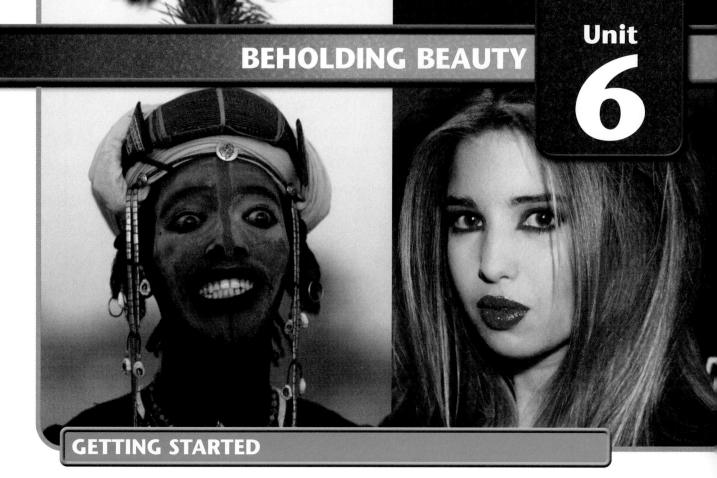

GETTING STARTED

Warm Up

The saying "Beauty is in the eye of the beholder" expresses the idea that there are no absolute standards of beauty. Beauty is judged differently according to each person's preferences.

1 Make a list of three well-known men and three well-known women you consider attractive. Work with a partner. Compare your lists and explain why you chose these people.

2 Both of the people in the pictures above are considered beautiful in their own cultures. List the similarities and the differences you find between them. Then work with a partner and compare and discuss your lists.

3 Listen to a conversation between a grandfather and grandson. What are they discussing? Compare your answer with your partner's.

Figure It Out

4 If you could create a man or woman to represent your society's physical ideal, what would he or she look like? Complete the questionnaire and compare your answers with a partner's. How do your descriptions differ?

The Ideal Man

1. If you could choose the height for the ideal man, he would be

    a. short   **b.** medium height   **c.** tall   **d.** very tall

2. Assuming that you could pick a body type for him, he would be

    a. slim   **b.** athletic   **c.** muscular   **d.** stocky

    If you could choose his hair color and style, would his hair be

    a. blond   **b.** black   **c.** brown   **d.** auburn

    Provided you had the chance to select his eye color, his eyes would be

    a. hazel   **b.** blue   **c.** brown   **d.** gray   **e.** black

3. If you opted for a skin type, his skin would be

    a. dark   **b.** tan   **c.** white   **d.** brown

    If you were to choose a facial shape for him, it would be

    a. square   **b.** oval   **c.** tapering   **d.** round

4. If you could decide on his facial hair, he would have

    a. nothing   **b.** a moustache   **c.** a goatee   **d.** a beard

The Ideal Woman

1. If you could choose the height for the ideal woman, she would be

    a. petite   **b.** medium height   **c.** tall   **d.** very tall

2. Provided that you could pick a body type for her, she would be

    a. slim   **b.** athletic   **c.** large

3. If you could choose her hair color and type, her hair would be

    a. blond   **b.** black   **c.** brown   **d.** auburn
    e. short   **f.** medium length   **g.** long   **h.** cropped
    i. straight   **j.** curly   **k.** wavy

4. Provided you were able to select her eye color, her eyes would be

    a. hazel   **b.** blue   **c.** brown   **d.** gray   **e.** black

5. If you were asked to opt for a skin type, her skin would be

    a. dark   **b.** tan   **c.** white   **d.** brown

6. If you were to choose a facial type for her, it would be

    a. square   **b.** heart-shaped   **c.** oval   **d.** round

7. Assuming you could decide on her mouth and lips, would you like her mouth to be

    a. small and thin   **b.** medium   **c.** large and full

---

☑ **⑤** **Vocabulary Check** Match the words on the left with their meanings on the right.

_____ **1.** stocky	**a.** wide forehead and tapering at the chin
_____ **2.** cropped	**b.** decide on
_____ **3.** hazel	**c.** greenish brown
_____ **4.** oval	**d.** short, pointed beard
_____ **5.** opt	**e.** short, strong, and solid in appearance
_____ **6.** goatee	**f.** tall and thin
_____ **7.** heart-shaped	**g.** shaped like an egg
	h. cut short

Talk About It

 6 A mother and daughter are discussing regrets. Work with a partner. Take turns being the mother and daughter and discuss the topics below. Use the conversation as a model.

ROLES	MODEL CONVERSATION	FUNCTIONS
Daughter:	If you were able to, how would you have changed your past?	Ask about a past regret.
Mother:	Let's see. I suppose I would have taken better care of my body. I would never have started smoking.	Mention two past regrets.
Daughter:	And if you had, what would be different?	Ask about a hypothetical situation.
Mother:	I wouldn't have a weight problem today, and I'd be in better health.	Speculate.

Topics

a. financial affairs   c. bad habits   e. family

b. career   d. relationships   f. (your own idea)

GRAMMAR

First Conditional and Second Conditional

Conditional sentences express conditions and wishes. They usually consist of a condition (an *if* clause) and a result clause. These clauses can be in either order. The first conditional is used to talk about events that may actually happen in the present or the future if a certain condition occurs.

Real Condition	Possible Result
If + simple present	simple present
If I don't use facial cream...	my face **feels** dry all day.
If + simple present	future
If I get bored with my hair...	**I'll dye** it bright orange/**I'm going to dye** it pink.

The second conditional is used to speculate about present unreal, impossible, or hypothetical conditions.

Unreal Present Condition	Hypothetical Result
If + past tense form	*would* + verb
If you **worked out** every day,	you **would be** in a much better shape now.

Unit 6

69

Third Conditional: Speculating About the Past

The third conditional is used to speculate about the past given unreal, impossible, or hypothetical past conditions. It is often used to express regret or criticism about past actions.

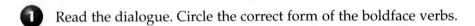

If + past perfect	*would, could, might + past participle*
If Vicki **hadn't gotten** her teeth fixed when she was 16,	she **wouldn't have won** that beauty contest.

1 Read the dialogue. Circle the correct form of the boldface verbs.

MARK: Hey, Linda, according to a global study, 65 percent of American women and 47 percent of American men think about their appearance all the time.

LINDA: Hmmm. I guess if I **(1.) was/were/will be/had been** American, I would really stick out because I'm not at all concerned with how I look. So who is in second place?

MARK: For women, it's Russia with 51 percent. But Olga is Russian, and she isn't into her looks that much. I guess if she had been raised in Russia, she **(2.) has probably gotten/would have probably gotten/will probably have gotten/had probably gotten** into that state of mind herself.

LINDA: Who's in second place for male vanity? Brazilians?

MARK: No, Mexican men, with 40 percent.

LINDA: Really? I **(3.) tell/told/will tell/had told** Roberto about that, if I don't forget. He's from Mexico.

MARK: But even if I hadn't read this, I **(4.) have still guessed/would still have guessed/will still have guessed/had still guessed** that Roberto is vain.

LINDA: With good reason, he's gorgeous. If we **(5.) aren't/weren't/wouldn't be/hadn't been** such good friends, and if he **(6.) doesn't have/didn't have/wouldn't have/hadn't have** a partner, he'd be in big trouble! So, what about the rest of the survey?

MARK: Well, it says the third vainest are Mexican women with 45 percent of those surveyed answering "yes."

LINDA: Wow! If I had known, I **(7.) have paid/would have paid/had paid/will have paid** more attention to my looks in Mexico!

2 Peter read about the study too. Read the article. Complete Peter's diary with the appropriate form of the verb in parenthesis.

IN A RECENT STUDY, researchers at Michigan State University looked at sixty-eight surveys, conducted over forty years and involving 5,000 subjects, to find out how physical appearance influences people's lives. The results showed that good-looking people earn more, get called on more in class, receive lighter court sentences, and are perceived as friendlier and more intelligent.

Dear Diary,

So, if you **(1. be)** _____ good-looking, your life **(2. be)**_____ much easier. How unfair! Look at me! If I **(3. be)** _____ taller, more athletic, and **(4. have)** _____ all my hair, I **(5. have)** _____ a much better life. If I **(6. work out)** _____ more in college and not just studied, I **(7. gain)** _____ all this weight. Yeah, but what about my hair? That's still falling out. If I **(8. have)** _____ the money, I **(9. can get)** _____ some hair implants. That **(10. be)** _____ a good start. And if I ever **(11. become)** _____ rich, I also **(12. get)** _____ my body worked on— add some muscles to my chest and have a tummy tuck. My face is OK, except for my nose. I **(13. keep)** _____ it the way it is if I **(14. can afford)** _____ to change it. The study says that attractive people get lighter court sentences as well. If I **(15. be)** _____ a hunk, I probably **(16. get away)** _____ without paying taxes. I wish! Oh well . . . But I'm happy and I adore my life. If I **(17. change)** _____ anything, I wouldn't be so happy!

3 Work with a partner. Take turns being Peter and his friend. Use the cues to complete their conversation.

Example:

FRIEND: What would you buy if you had a million dollars?

PETER: If I had a million dollars, I'd buy a Rolex watch, a solid gold pinky ring, platinum shirt buttons, and a tie clip with a huge diamond on it.

FRIEND: What else would you do?

    a. face lift and tummy tuck   **d.** sail around the world

    b. brand-new wardrobe   **e.** penthouse on Park Avenue

    c. very expensive car   **f.** (your own idea)

Unit 6

4 Peter came into an inheritance and became a millionaire. Peter is discussing his plans with his mother. She always believes things will go wrong. Work with a partner. Take turns being Peter and his mother.

Example:

MOTHER: What if your jewelry turns out to be fake?

PETER: If my jewelry turns out to be fake, I'll hire the best lawyer in town and sue the jeweler .

    a. wrinkles and weight gain   **d.** lose your boat

    b. clothes don't fit   **e.** your penthouse is robbed

    c. crash your car   **f.** (your own idea)

Other Expressions with the Conditional

Though not all conditional clauses contain the word *if*, their function is the same. *(Just) in case* and *in the (unlikely) event that* are used to express the possibility that something will happen.

> I'll need to buy some new clothes, **just in case** I decide to move to the Caribbean.
>
> **In the event that** we sign a contract, you'll be moved to New York.

5 Combine the sentences to form a single sentence with the same meaning. Use *in case* or *in the event that*.

Example: Most likely you won't have time to go shopping with me, but you might be able to make time. If so, I'll give you the name of the store.

I'll give you the name of the store in case you have time to come along with me.

    a. Most likely you don't want to get a tattoo, but maybe you do. If so, I'll give you the name of a tattoo place that's safe.

    b. The wounds after your surgery will most likely heal in ten to fourteen days, but maybe they won't. If so, you will have to return to the hospital.

    c. I don't think my friend has this CD, but maybe he does. If so, can I exchange it?

    d. You probably don't want to cut your hair, but if you do, I can recommend a very good hairdresser.

We use *only if* and *as long as* to indicate that meeting this condition is necessary for the action to happen. When the *only if* appears in the initial position, the subject and the auxiliary verb of the result clause are inverted with no meaning change.

> We'll go to the museum **only if** the body art exhibition is still on.
>
> You can get a tattoo **as long as** it's a small one.
>
> **Only if** I see dramatic results **will** I **stay on** this horrible diet.

6 Check Your Understanding Check the conditionals that you are *most likely* to use in these different situations.

	First Conditional	Second Conditional	Third Conditional
a. You are talking about all your missed opportunities.	☐	☐	☐
b. You are discussing the consequences of winning the lottery.	☐	☐	☐
c. You are planning your trip to a health spa.	☐	☐	☐
d. You are criticizing your brother's way of raising his kids.	☐	☐	☐

7 Express Yourself Work with a partner. Choose one of the situations above and write a dialogue. Perform your dialogue for another pair.

LISTENING and SPEAKING

Listen: The Beauty of Symmetry

1 Before You Listen What helps you decide if an object or person is beautiful? Its shape? Proportions? Color? Texture? Compare your ideas with a partner's.

STRATEGY **Recognizing Cause and Effect** When listening for critical analysis, it is important to recognize relationships between ideas, such as cause and effect. Focusing on expressions such as, *as if, in case of, in the event that, only if, as long as, on condition that, provided that,* and *assuming that,* will help you identify and analyze these relationships.

2 Listen to a lecture on the relationship between symmetry and beauty. Summarize the main ideas. Compare your summary with a partner's.

3 Listen again and complete the chart.

Main Idea	Summary
general definition of symmetry	
example of bilateral symmetry	
example of radial symmetry	

Pronunciation

4 Predict the intonation pattern of the boldface words. Write arrows above each word.

a. **A:** Look at **that**! This ad claims that they can make you lose seventy pounds in just a week. What a joke!

B: **Really**? I'd like that! What's their phone number?

A: Oh, **great**! You're actually going to fall for it?

B: You've gotta **try** it before you knock it. And look at this! She looks *great*!

A: Oh, **really**? It looks to me like she could put on a few.

b. **A:** **Fantastic**! I won a workout machine in the raffle at work.

B: What do you mean, **fantastic**? I think it's **fantastic**!

A: Except, I hate working out.

B: **Wonderful**! Just give it to me. I love working out.

A: Well, have fun for me.

B: No pain, no gain.

5 Listen to the passage to check your predictions.

6 Work with a partner. Take turns reading the conversations, focusing on the intonation of the boldfaced words.

Speak Out

 Keeping on Track In an effective discussion, speakers remain on the topic. When speakers digress, acknowledge what they've said politely, and then move back to the topic.

Polite Ways of Keeping the Discussion on Track:

That's an interesting idea, but it raises a different point. Could we come back to it later?

That's a good idea, but let's get back to it later...

I think that's a point worth discussing, but let's finish this issue before moving onto a different one.

That's a valid point, but it's getting off the subject. Right now we're talking about...

 Work in groups of three. Discuss some of the following topics according to the diagram.

• body art	• body painting	• makeup	• cosmetic dentistry
• tattoos	• body building	• hairstyles	• cosmetic surgery
• body piercing	• latest fashions	• models	

(Make a statement about the topic.) → (Elaborate on the topic.) → (Digress.) → (Bring the conversation back on track.)

READING and WRITING

Read About It

 Before You Read How often do you buy hair or skin products? Clothing? How much money do you spend on improving your appearance in a year?

 Evaluating Supporting Examples When reading critically, efficient readers look for examples that the author has used to support the main points. A good reader constantly observes whether claims are supported with related examples and evaluates the relevance of the examples.

 Read the article on page 76. As you read, note two examples and one general statement. Compare your list with a partner's.

Our Obsession with Beauty
By Montserrat Fernandez Pinkley

"Beauty is everywhere a welcome guest."
-Johann Wolfgang von Goethe

Human beings have always been fascinated by beauty, and while its definition varies, its pursuit spans centuries and continents. The perception of what is
5 beautiful changes, sometimes drastically, with each culture, each time period, and even each individual, which begs the question, why pursue something so elusive?

"Beauty is as relative as light and dark."
—Paul Klee

When deciding what, or more importantly,
10 who is beautiful, each society has its own standards, which are dictated by a series of cultural, biological, and political factors. Since these factors vary widely across cultures, it makes sense that the idea of beauty does too.
15 The modern, Western view of a beautiful woman is tall, slender, and young, with shiny hair. There are parts of the world, however, where it is just the opposite. In some non-Western societies, such as the Tuareg of the
20 Sahara, obesity is considered beautiful. Other African societies equate beauty with an elongated neck or an enlarged lower lip, while in some parts of East Asia, small feet are considered beautiful. Even Western societies
25 in times past had a very different ideal of beauty than what it is currently in vogue. In Victorian times, a pale complexion, a waif-like body, and an unnaturally wide forehead were things to admire, while during the 17th
30 century, a round figure and rosy cheeks were the desired features.

"If you get simple beauty and nought else, you get about the best thing God invents."
—Robert Browning

Making yourself beautiful is not always an easy task. For centuries, people have altered their bodies in order to fit the accepted ideal
35 of beauty. In ancient Egypt, luxurious hair was considered beautiful; both men and women would shave their

heads only to cover them with a wig, which would often be dyed red, blue, or black and
40 then scented with perfume. The Egyptians also were one of the first documented civilizations to have used makeup and perfume. Egyptian women would paint their cheeks using ocher, and they also decorated their eyes with
45 malachite, a copper ore, which would give their eyes the color which symbolized fertility— green. The ancient Greeks and Romans also enhanced their beauty with cosmetics and fragrances. Greek women would paint their
50 faces, while Romans would use oil-based perfumes in their baths, their fountains, and even on their weapons. The Mayans would file their teeth and decorate them with various semi-precious stones, such as jade and onyx.
55 However, the Aztecs preferred beautification through scent, often wearing fragrant garlands of gardenias around their necks, to the Mayan's beautiful smile.

Obsession with personal appearance was
60 also equally widespread among the European aristocracy in times past. Montesquieu, the French essayist, wrote: "There is nothing more serious than the goings-on in the morning when Madam is taking care of her
65 grooming." But men of the 18th century, wearing their wigs of cascading curls, stockings and high heels to show off their legs, scented gloves, and rouge, were equally self-absorbed. "Men have their color, powder
70 puffs, pomades, and perfumes," noted one lady socialite," and it occupies them just as much as or even more than women." Victorian women would pluck their foreheads in order to make them wider and therefore more
75 beautiful. The Tuareg of the Sahara are known to force-feed their women balls of bread in order to make them beautifully obese, while in the United States girls and women diet and starve in order to achieve the current ideal of
80 a slender figure.

"Personal beauty is a greater recommendation than any letter of reference."
—Aristotle

A lot of time is spent in improving our appearance, but to what end? Is it in our best interest to be beautiful, or is the pursuit of beauty in vain? According to recent studies, it seems that being beautiful carries certain advantages. Beautiful people tend to have more attractive husbands or wives. They are thought to be more intelligent and sociable by their teachers, they have an easier time finding jobs, and they are treated more leniently in front of a court of law. The reason for this seems to be that beauty and survival are closely linked. Beautiful people are subconsciously registered as being healthier and more fit. Apparently, a youthful, symmetrical appearance free of blemishes (which are the only standards of beauty that have remained constant throughout time) is what helped our prehistoric ancestors choose a mate and ensure the survival of the species. A youthful, symmetrical appearance meant that there was no obvious disability or disease that would result in premature death. The human race, and arguably all of nature, is genetically engineered to look for and appreciate beauty. In fact, our lives depend on it!

3 Answer the questions. Then work with a partner and compare your answers.

   a. What time periods and countries or ethnic groups does the author cover in the article?

   b. In the 18th century, what was the attitude of the aristocratic French male to beautification?

   c. What conclusion does the author reach about why we seek out beauty?

4 On a separate piece of paper, write supporting examples from the reading for each general statement.

   a. When deciding who is beautiful, each society has its own standards.

   b. For centuries people have altered their bodies in order to fit the accepted ideal of beauty.

   c. It seems that being beautiful carries certain advantages.

☑ **5** **Vocabulary Check** Match the words on the left with their meanings on the right.

_____ **1.** begs the question (line 7)	**a.** fragile-looking child
_____ **2.** elusive (line 8)	**b.** ring of flowers
_____ **3.** waif (line 27)	**c.** overweight
_____ **4.** ore (line 45)	**d.** difficult to understand
_____ **5.** file (line 52)	**e.** extremely thin
_____ **6.** garland (line 56)	**f.** avoids the issue
_____ **7.** obese (lines 20, 77)	**g.** mildly
_____ **8.** leniently (line 91)	**h.** rock used for minerals
	i. sharpen

Think About It

6 Work in small groups. Discuss the meanings of the italicized sayings in the reading and the values behind them.

Write: Writing Supporting Paragraphs

 An effective essay contains a body of two to four support paragraphs. These paragraphs support the main point, or thesis statement, which appears in the introductory paragraph. Each supporting paragraph should discuss one aspect of the topic, and each supporting paragraph should have its own topic sentence that clearly states the main idea of the paragraph.

 Read the essay below. Then answer the questions that follow.

> ### Are Skin Products Helpful?
>
> Many people spend a lot of money on skin products in the belief that they will look younger. But are these products really helpful? Research shows that many expensive skin products cost only pennies to make. Moreover, dermatologists say that the ingredients in these products may actually make the skin age faster. As a result, your investment in skin care problems may be hurting not only your bank account but also your complexion.
>
> When people buy expensive skin products, often what they're paying for are fancy containers. They're also paying for the high cost of marketing, for the commercials and magazine ads that promote the products. In fact, the ingredients in the products that help keep the skin smooth cost very little. People can buy the same-quality skin care products by purchasing less expensive or generic brands. They can also can make their own skin care products by combining inexpensive ingredients purchased at the drugstore or supermarket.
>
> People also need to be aware of the ingredients in the skin products they buy. Some of them may be harmful to their skin. Dermatologists have found that one popular anti-aging ingredient works by peeling off the outer layer of skin. In some people, this may cause redness, blistering, and increased sensitivity to the sun. This in turn may cause increased wrinkling.
>
> When choosing skin products, people need to think carefully about two things. First, is the cost of the product worth it? Second, how will the product affect their skin? They may be surprised at what they find.

    a. What is the main point of the essay? Underline the thesis statement.

    b. How many supporting paragraphs are in the essay?

    c. What is the main idea of each supporting paragraph? Underline the topic sentences.

Write About It

 Choose one of the topics from the box, narrow it, and write an introductory paragraph about it. Then write two paragraphs that support the thesis statement.

> • beauty products
> • body image
> • inner beauty
> • (your own idea)

  Check Your Writing Exchange papers with a partner. Use the questions below to give feedback to your partner. When you get your own paper back, revise as necessary.

> • Is the thesis statement clear?
> • Do the paragraphs support the thesis statement?
> • Does each paragraph have a topic sentence that states the main idea of the paragraph?

PROGRESS CHECK

GRAMMAR

> **USING TIME EFFECTIVELY** It is important not to spend too much time on one question. You can come back to it if you need to. When you identify the incorrect part of the sentence, circle the answer and move quickly onto the next sentence. The important thing is to detect the error.

A Each sentence has four underlined words or phrases. One of these underlined words or phrases is incorrect. Circle the letter of the word or phrase that is incorrect.

1. I regretted <u>to leave</u> my job at I.B.M. and going <u>to work</u> for a dot-com **Ⓐ B C D**
           A   **B**

   start-up company because the dot-com stopped <u>making</u> money soon
                                                C

   after I <u>had been offered</u> a job with them.
             D

2. Only if you really loved <u>to travel</u>, <u>you would want</u> to be a pilot because **A B C D**
                            A   **B**

   pilots are required <u>to travel</u> several days in a row <u>without stopping</u>.
                   C   **D**

3. I <u>invited</u> to be a professional "laugher" for a TV show a few years ago, **A B C D**
     A

   but unfortunately, <u>laughing</u> was not my ticket to stardom because
                   B

   it was essential <u>to be able to</u> laugh in a variety of ways, and
                 C

   I <u>was unable</u> to do that.
      D

4. If I <u>had just stayed</u> with Nike, <u>I'd</u> probably <u>have been promoted</u> to a **A B C D**
         A   **B**   **C**

   great job in management by now and <u>have been making</u> a lot
                                       D

   of money today.

5. I didn't <u>start acting</u> in TV commercials until I was in my seventies **A B C D**
            A

   when I <u>was heard</u> about an acting course for senior citizens. Now, if
           B

   I <u>told</u> you how much fun that job was, you just <u>wouldn't believe</u> me.
    C   **D**

6. I tell everyone I meet that a job this easy <u>shouldn't be allowed</u>, but   **A B C D**

                                             A

   luckily for me, it is. I'm a hand model, and as long as my hands

   <u>remaining</u> as beautiful as they are, <u>I'm told</u> that <u>I'll continue</u> working.

  B   **C**   **D**

7. If I <u>have imagined</u> how <u>to make</u> money as a hot air balloonist   **A B C D**

            A   **B**

   on my own, that's exactly what I <u>would have been doing</u> all these years.

                                          C

   Unfortunately, I <u>wasn't made</u> aware of the possibilities until it was too late.

                      D

8. Some career counselors <u>are known</u> for <u>encouraging</u> people to follow   **A B C D**

                             A   **B**

   their dreams. But what people need is <u>to advise</u> <u>on adjusting</u> their

                                          C   **D**

   dreams to make them fit the current job market.

STRATEGY | **LOOKING FOR CLUES** Look for grammatical clues in the question. These might include time words, the tenses of other verbs, or subject verb-agreement (a singular subject needs a singular verb form). When you identify the correct answer, circle it and move quickly to the next question.

B Circle the letter of the correct answer to complete each sentence.

1. Schools today _____ places of conflict and fear   **A B (C) D**
   for some students.
   - **(A)** will be
   - **(B)** are being
   - **(C)** can be
   - **(D)** has been

2. If a student is full of fear, he or she _____ difficulty   **A B C D**
   concentrating.
   - **(A)** has had
   - **(B)** will have
   - **(C)** had
   - **(D)** have

3. In order to create safer learning environments, conflict resolution   **A B C D**
   programs _____ to teach students how to resolve their
   problems productively and nonviolently.
   - **(A)** will create
   - **(B)** have created
   - **(C)** were being created
   - **(D)** have been created

4. Students who have learned alternatives to violence and anger
in the school environment often _____ those skills in the
workplace and the community at large when they become adults.   A B C D
   (A) had started to use   **(C)** start to use
   (B) starting to use   **(D)** start to using

5. Many believe that if all students had been taught conflict resolution
skills from an early age, many of the recent problems in our
schools _____.   A B C D
   (A) could have been prevented   **(C)** can prevent
   (B) could have prevented   **(D)** can be prevented

6. Conflict resolution programs encourage students _____ to
solve their problems collectively and collaboratively.   A B C D
   (A) attempting   **(C)** be attempted
   (B) attempted   **(D)** to attempt

VOCABULARY

MAKING AN EDUCATED GUESS If you do not know the meaning of the word, look for
clues in the context of the sentence. Try to eliminate one or more choices, then your
chances of guessing will be better. Making educated guesses can be an effective
test-taking strategy.

A Circle the letter of the word that can best replace the **boldface** word
in each sentence.

1. A common **grievance** of teens through the ages is that their parents
don't seem to appreciate their children's sense of style.   A B ⓒ D
   (A) issue   **(C)** complaint
   (B) trouble   **(D)** problem

2. Many believe that women who wear excessive amounts of makeup
are attempting to **disguise** their true selves.   A B C D
   (A) conceal   **(C)** improve
   (B) explore   **(D)** change

3. For some, the **allure** of a beautiful person comes from the mystery of
what isn't seen or known about that person rather than what is.   A B C D
   (A) grace   **(C)** deception
   (B) beauty   **(D)** attraction

4. After Marta got up and walked out of the room, her beauty and her **lingering** presence made the others feel uncomfortable discussing openly what they'd heard about her.   A B C D
   - (A) timely
   - (B) gigantic
   - (C) habitual
   - (D) remaining

5. Pete's **lofty** principles wouldn't permit him to let his employees take the brunt of his financial loss.   A B C D
   - (A) high
   - (B) humble
   - (C) foolish
   - (D) selfish

> **STRATEGY** **ANSWERING WORD FORMATION VOCABULARY QUESTIONS** Some exams test your ability to change words so that they fit into a sentence grammatically. Be sure to examine the sentence to determine what part of speech (noun, verb, adverb) is needed to fill the blank before you change the word. Review the suffixes so you can use the base form to create other parts of speech.

B The words on the right can be used to form a word that fits in the blank grammatically. Complete each sentence with the correct form of the word.

1. The manager of the company had a very _threatening_ manner during the contract negotiations.   **THREATEN**

2. Some people feel that wearing expensive clothing and driving expensive cars is a true _____ of success.   **VALIDATE**

3. Some women feel that society puts too much _____ on looking "good" and too little on acting "good."   **EMPHASIZE**

4. There is a strong _____ among some people that good looks can help you get a job.   **BELIEVE**

5. In my opinion, I'd rather work with someone who's _____ than work with someone who's incompetent and good-looking.   **FRIEND**

GETTING STARTED

Warm Up

1 The people in the pictures are all left-handed. Work in small groups. Brainstorm common difficulties left-handed people encounter. Then rank them from the most to the least serious.

2 Are you left-handed, or do you know someone who is?

3 Listen to two friends discuss problems that left-handed people encounter. What difficulties do they mention?

Figure It Out

4 Hidden beliefs that we hold are often reflected in the language we use. Read about the expressions that we use to describe left and right on the next page.

The English language is filled with expressions that reveal bias against all things left. Negative associations which suggest that left-handers are wrong in some
5 essential way are embedded in the language. For example, someone who has been rejected has been *left out*. A person whose ideas are considered irrelevant, extreme, or crazy is said to be *out in left field*. The bad dancer whom
10 everyone dreads as a partner is described as having *two left feet*. An unfavorable remark is called a *left-handed compliment*. This bias applies to borrowed words as well. For example, the English word *sinister*, which
15 means "evil or threatening," is derived from a Latin word meaning merely "the left side."

Someone who is vulgar, tasteless, or lacking grace in social situations is *gauche*. This word comes from the French word of the same
20 spelling with the neutral meaning of "left."

In contrast, *right* is synonymous with positive things. The word *right* itself is readily associated with whatever is morally or socially correct, legal, and just. The person
25 who conducts himself in an exemplary manner is seen by some as *righteous*, and by some as *Mr. Right*. An essential employee is known as the boss' *right-hand*. And, of course, the *right-thinking* student who
30 has read this article is *on the right track* to understanding how bias is embedded in the language we use every day!

 5 **Vocabulary Check** Match the expressions on the left with their meanings on the right.

_____ **1.** reveal (line 2)   **a.** to be fearful of

_____ **2.** bias (line 2)   **b.** fixed or located within something

_____ **3.** embedded (line 5)   **c.** make visible, disclose

_____ **4.** dread (line 10)   **d.** strong feelings for or against something

_____ **5.** derive (line 15)   **e.** having almost the same meaning as

_____ **6.** synonymous (line 21)   **f.** come from, proceed from

_____ **7.** exemplary (line 25)   **g.** highly exaggerated

      h. serving as a desirable model or example

Talk About It

6 A pollster is conducting a survey about left-handedness. Work with a partner. Take turns being the pollster and the respondent, and discuss the issues on the next page. Use the conversation as a model.

Example: products that are designed for left-handers

ROLES	MODEL CONVERSATION	FUNCTIONS
Pollster:	As a left-hander, what products would make your life easier?	Ask a question.
Respondent:	Well, a guitar that is made for lefties would certainly help. It is very awkward to play a guitar meant for right-handers.	Answer the question and give details.
Pollster:	So musicians who are left-handed need guitars, mandolins, and other instruments designed just for them?	Ask a follow-up question.
Respondent:	Of course! And the people who design office equipment and power tools have to think of our comfort and safety, too. Tools which are made with only right-handers in mind cause a lot of accidents.	Answer the question and elaborate.

<u>Issues</u>

a. situations in which a left-hander may be forced to use his right hand

b. professions that might discriminate against left-handed people

c. situations in which being left-handed is an advantage

d. (your own idea)

GRAMMAR

Adjective Clauses

Adjective clauses, also called relative clauses, are used to define or give more information about a noun or an indefinite pronoun (*the one, someone, something*). They directly follow the noun or pronoun they refer to. They are generally introduced by relative pronouns such as *that, which, who, whom,* or *whose.*

> main clause   adjective clause—defines the kind of article
> ⌐Ana is reading an article⌐<u>that discusses bias against left-handers</u>.
>
> main ...   adjective clause—defines the class of left-handers   ... clause
> ⌐Left-handers⌐<u>who are forced to use their right hand often</u>⌐have learning problems⌐

1   Underline the adjective clauses in the article on page 84. Compare your answers with a partner's.

A relative pronoun can be the subject or the object of the adjective clause. When it is the subject, it precedes the verb phrase of the adjective clause.

Subject of the Adjective Clause

      subject   verb phrase
Musicians <u>who are left-handed</u> have difficulty finding instruments.

        subject verb phrase
I know of a few companies <u>that manufacture products for left-handers</u>.

Object of the Adjective Clause

      object subject + verb phrase
Here is the book about ambidexterity <u>*that* my friend gave me</u>.

    object subject + verb
The musician <u>whom you met</u> plays a left-handed guitar.

In informal speech, it is common to omit the relative pronoun when it is the **object** of the adjective clause.

Here is the book about ambidexterity [that] my friend gave me.

The musician [whom] you met plays a left-handed guitar.

2 Combine the sentences using the correct relative pronoun. Use the second sentence as an adjective clause.

Example: The catalogue for left-handers is great.   I got it in the mail yesterday.
    <u>*The catalogue for left-handers that I got in the mail yesterday is great.*</u>

  a. The company has expanded.   It makes left-handed products.
  b. That man owns the factory.   You saw him shopping yesterday.
  c. That worker is left-handed.   He had an accident.
  d. Power tools can be dangerous for lefties.   They are made for right-handers.
  e. The insurance plan had better be good!   The company has it.

Identifying and Non-Identifying Adjective Clauses

Identifying adjective clauses provide essential information about a noun or an indefinite pronoun. They identify or define the person or thing in question. They are not separated by commas from the main clause.

The man <u>who compiled the list of famous left-handers</u> is over there. (which man?)

I bought a copy of the book <u>that he wrote</u>. (which book?)

Non-identifying adjective clauses provide additional information about a noun or pronoun. They do not identify or define; they simply tell us more about the person or thing in question. Non-identifying adjective clauses are separated by commas. *That* cannot be used in a non-identifying clause.

> Tom Cruise, <u>who is left-handed</u>, is a well-known actor.
>
> Another famous left-hander is Michelangelo, <u>who lived in the 16th century</u>.

3 Work with a partner. Decide if the adjective clauses in these sentences are **I** (identifying) or **N** (non-identifying) clauses. Add commas where necessary.

_____ **a.** Guns that are designed for right-handers are a problem for left-handers.

_____ **b.** Left-handers who use them to hunt or shoot have a higher rate of accidents.

_____ **c.** Guns which are dangerous for right-handers too are a big problem today.

_____ **d.** Countries that don't allow everyone to own a gun have a much lower rate of accidents.

_____ **e.** Children who are often curious are the primary victims of handguns stored in the home.

_____ **f.** Laws that control the use of guns are a good idea for everybody.

Adjective Clauses with *Whose*

Whose is used to show possession. *Whose* + a noun is used to introduce an adjective clause that serves to identify or define a noun or pronoun in the main clause. *Whose* cannot be omitted.

> possessor   object possessed
> The artist   *whose* painting I admire   is ambidextrous.
>
> possessors   object possessed
> I met with the students   *whose* articles about bias   were published.

4 Combine the pairs of sentences using *whose*. Use the second sentence as an adjective clause and add commas as needed.

a. The professor gave an excellent lecture.   His research is on handedness.

b. The student took great notes.   I borrowed her notes.

c. I thanked the student for her notes.   I copied her notes.

d. The professor called on me.   I missed his class.

e. The professor appreciated my comments.   I answered his question.

f. A classmate found my notebook.   I have her phone number.

5 **Check Your Understanding** Complete each sentence with an adjective clause. Compare your completed sentences with a partner's.

a. A lefty is a person who _____ is left-handed. _____

b. An ideal dancing partner is a person whose _____

c. Bias in language is something that _____

d. The sculptor whom _____

e. School desks which _____

f. Handedness is a concept that _____

 6 **Express Yourself** Work with a partner. Write a dialogue for one of the situations below, and perform your dialogue for another pair.

a. At a crowded party you need to point out your new boss to the person you came with.

b. You are explaining to a coworker why it is that you haven't yet finished the project you are working on.

c. You see a friend on the street who owes you money, and you want to collect it.

d. You are explaining what you like to do in your free time to a party guest.

e. You have just attended a fabulous concert, and you want to tell a friend about it.

LISTENING and SPEAKING

Listen: Write Right!

1 **Before You Listen** Look at the pictures. Which one is closest to the way you hold your hand when you write? What significance do you think this may have?

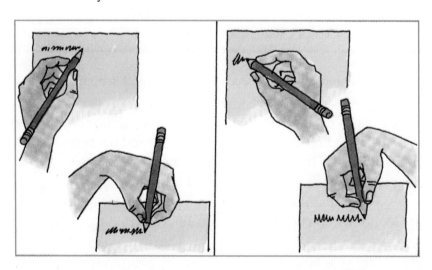

Listening to Summarize An effective listener focuses on the key idea when summarizing a conversation or lecture. Very few, if any, examples and details are included. A good summary provides a brief overview of content.

2 Listen to a lecture about the role of the brain in writing. Check the statement that best summarizes the main idea.

_____ **a.** Left-handed writers are the exact reverse of right-handed writers, as shown in recent research on the brain.

_____ **b.** Research has shown that some people write in the "hook" position due to genetic disposition.

_____ **c.** There is a relationship between writing position and location of the language function in the right or left hemisphere.

 3 Listen again and complete the chart. What have you learned that helps you understand your own brain? Share your ideas with a partner.

Main Ideas	Supporting Information
Possible significance of writing in the "hook" position	
Percentage of left-handers who have their language centers in the right hemisphere of the brain	

Pronunciation

In casual connected speech, a sound that is pronounced one way in isolation can be pronounced differently when it appears next to certain other sounds. This sound change can take place within a word or between two words.

Sound in Isolation	Sound Affected by the Presence of Another Sound
force + past tense –d	*forced* pronounced /**t**/ because of /**s**/ in force
forced + to	/**t**/ in *forced* pronounced once and held a little longer because of /**t**/ beginning the word *to*
Example: As a child in school, I was **forced to** use my right hand.	

4 Work with a partner. Predict which sounds in the boldfaced words will be affected by another sound nearby.

    a. At school, I was **asked to write** with my right hand.

    b. My teacher **said you should use** both hands if possible.

    c. **Could you** write with your other hand?

    d. I know **what you're** thinking, he said.

    e. Do you **want to** watch me type with my toes?

5 Listen to the sentences to check your predictions.

6 Work with a partner. Take turns saying the sentences, focusing on sound changes.

Speak Out

STRATEGY **Keeping a Discussion Going** The person leading a discussion usually monitors the progress of the meeting. The discussion leader tries to determine if a point has not been discussed thoroughly or if the participants have not contributed as much as they should have. In this case, direct encouragement is appropriate, either by the leader or by other group members.

Encourage Elaboration	
Could you please elaborate on your ideas a little more?	(more depth and detail needed to cover the subject thoroughly)
Encourage Participation	
Julia, we haven't heard your opinion on the issue of handwriting training yet. What do you think?	(group member has not yet contributed ideas or comments)

7 Decide if these expressions are used to **E** (encourage elaboration) or **P** (encourage participation). Compare your answers with a partner's.

    _____ **1.** I'd appreciate your expanding on that idea, Peter.

    _____ **2.** I believe we've heard from everyone except Anne.

    _____ **3.** Who could take that idea to the next level?

    _____ **4.** I feel we haven't covered the topic in depth.

    _____ **5.** We'd love to hear what you have to say, Kumiko.

    _____ **6.** That's the overview—now let's fill in the specific details.

    _____ **7.** Let's give Virginia a chance to comment on that.

    _____ **8.** How about it, Martin? What do you think?

    _____ **9.** We've just touched on the deeper implications of the problem.

    _____ **10.** Stuart, can you help us out here?

8 Work in a group. The purpose of your meeting is to plan and design a poster to increase public awareness of the needs of the differently-abled. Decide what text, attention-getting technique, and art you will use for your poster. Use appropriate expressions to keep the discussion going when necessary.

READING and WRITING

Read About It

1 **Before You Read** Do you think most cultures have a preference for handedness? Why?

STRATEGY **Identifying Generalizations** When reading for critical analysis, efficient readers pay attention to generalizations, statements presented as true and representative of a large category but based on limited or incomplete evidence. They also watch for qualifying statements. These are expressions writers use to protect themselves when not every example, generalization, conclusion, or reference can be supported to the same degree such as *some believe it is likely that . . .* and *no one quite knows why. . . .*

2 Read the passage. As you read, underline generalizations and examples of qualifying statements.

Life in the Left Lane

by Karen Odom

What's right about being left-handed? Apparently not too much, if statistics are any indication. Several studies show that a disproportionate number of people who
5 are left-handed are more apt to be accident prone, to be dyslexic, to stutter, and to suffer from migraine headaches. Take Carol, for example. She is forever bumping elbows with the person sitting next to her at lunch
10 and having to take off her watch (which she must wear on her right wrist) to wind or adjust it. To top it off, she
15 has been coping with migraine headaches for as long as she can remember.

Pablo Picasso

(continued on next page)

Carol isn't alone though. She is representative
20 of the estimated 10 to 13 percent of the world
population who happen to be left-handed.
Whether they are known as left-handers, lefties,
sinistrals, or southpaws, these people constantly
struggle to fit into a world that is dominated by
25 the right-handed. Forced to switch to the right
hand or to use awkward movements for such
ordinary things as starting a car, opening
a refrigerator door, pushing the button on a
water fountain, or simply opening a can of
30 beans, they do daily battle armed with large
amounts of patience and, mostly, good humor.

A sense of humor is definitely an advantage
when left-handers discover the large body
of myths, inaccuracies, and stereotypes that
35 right-handers seem all too willing to believe.
In the not-too-distant past, defenseless
children were accused of following the devil
or communism simply by virtue of using their
left hand. Left-handed women were sometimes
40 burned at the stake as witches. Other
unfortunates found their left hands covered
in leather mittens and tied behind their backs
until they surrendered to right-hand rule. Even
today, there are still some parents and
45 teachers who are committed to changing their
left-handed charges over to the right through
threats and punishment. And some people
persist in describing left-handers as oddballs
who are at best clumsy, unstable, rebellious,
50 or unintelligent. But the hardest pill to swallow
surely must be the much-cited studies
whose results point to shorter life spans
for left-handers.

The possibility that left-handers might have
55 a higher mortality rate has been supported
by several scientists. Two psychologists
recently reported this disturbing finding
in the *New England Journal of Medicine* after
studying the records of hand preference
60 of 987 deceased men and women in southern
California. On the average, those who were
right-handed lived to the age of seventy-five,
nine years longer than those who were left-
handed. Having found that women generally

65 live longer than
men, regardless
of hand preference,
the researchers went
on to discover that the
70 right-handed had
an additional five-year
advantage over those
whom fate had dealt
a left hand. And right-

Oprah Winfrey

75 handed men outlived left-handed men
by a full ten years! Although the psychologists
have no conclusive evidence, they assign the
differences in life span to a higher propensity
for fatal accidents among left-handers. Others
80 speculate that left-handers are depressed and
therefore more likely to commit suicide, that
they are at much greater risk due to the use
of power tools and industrial equipment made
for right-handers, and even that they may have
85 faulty immune systems.

Left-handedness has been a frustrating subject
of study and analysis for ages. Despite ongoing
studies, researchers don't know exactly why
certain characteristics can be attributed
90 to people who are left-handed. And neither
do we know why the overwhelming majority
of people around the world favor the right hand
over the left, regardless of race, sex, or culture.
(And, surprisingly, we aren't the only species
95 that feels that way! In the late 1800s, Pasteur
discovered that many living things have
a handedness preference. Some plants, like
the trumpet honeysuckle, wind to the right;
while others, such as bindweed, wind
100 to the left. Even seashells and toads have
a handedness preference.)

There are still a great number of questions
which require answers: Why aren't an equal
number of people left-handed and right-
105 handed? Why is it so rare that someone is truly
ambidextrous? What do migraine headaches
have to do with hand preference? Why do 80
percent of mothers around the world carry
their babies on the left? Some scientists doubt
110 we will ever know with certainty.

But life in the left lane isn't *all* bad. According to some brain researchers, the corpus callosum, which is the bridge between the two halves of the brain, is statistically more
115 likely to be thicker in left-handers. This, the theory goes, results in more efficient information transfer and redundancy in their brains. Many left-handers also demonstrate greater flexibility in terms of where language skills
120 are located in their brains, which results in a better recovery rate for left-handers who have a stroke or brain and head injuries. In addition, left-handers are generally more flexible in their hand usage than right-handers,
125 perhaps because they have had to deal with such a strongly right-oriented world. Consider, for example, the world of sports, where left-handed tennis players and baseball pitchers

have an advantage. Need we do more than
130 mention sports greats such as John McEnroe, Martina Navratilova, Ty Cobb, and Babe Ruth? And speaking of famous names, other talented left-handers who have left their print on the world include Julius Caesar,
135 Pablo Picasso, Oprah Winfrey, Paul McCartney, Judy Garland, Albert Einstein, Benjamin Franklin, Bruce Willis, and Whoopi Goldberg, to name just a few!

And the final good news for left-handers
140 is that the world is slowly becoming more accommodating. Items designed specifically for left-handers—like scissors, soup ladles with spouts on both sides, and guitars—are gradually helping make
145 the world right—at last—for lefties!

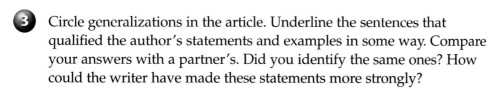

3 Circle generalizations in the article. Underline the sentences that qualified the author's statements and examples in some way. Compare your answers with a partner's. Did you identify the same ones? How could the writer have made these statements more strongly?

 4 **Vocabulary Check** Match the words on the left with their meanings on the right.

_____ **1.** apt to (line 5)   **a.** defective, weakened

_____ **2.** struggle (line 24)   **b.** duplication, repetition

_____ **3.** span (line 52)   **c.** give up hope

_____ **4.** disturbing (line 57)   **d.** causing worry or fear

_____ **5.** deceased (line 60)   **e.** likely to, inclined to

_____ **6.** faulty (line 85)   **f.** dead, no longer living

_____ **7.** redundancy (line 117)   **g.** fight, battle

h. period of time, range

Think About It

 5 Some people say that left-handers tend to be among the top intellectuals, musicians, and artists, despite their small numbers. Can you think of any evidence to support this idea? Can you think of any other group this stereotype applies to?

Write: Concluding Paragraphs

 STRATEGY Just as the introduction to an analytical essay presents the main argument, the conclusion restates the thesis, summarizes the main ideas, and provides closure for the essay. Common ways to end an essay include posing a question directly to the reader, making a prediction of some kind, or making a recommendation. A particularly eloquent quotation from an authority may also be used.

 Read the concluding paragraph of an essay on forced right-handedness. How does the author construct the conclusion? What features in it are similar to the features of an introductory paragraph? How did the author make the ending memorable?

> In conclusion, it is clear that forcing left-handed children to write with their right hands is both physically and emotionally harmful. As current research shows, this practice can result in dyslexia and stuttering, as well as depression, lack of self-esteem, and frustration so great that it leads to hatred of writing and other schoolwork. We as teachers have committed ourselves to foster a love of learning and a growing sense of self-worth and independence in our students. How, then, can we continue to undermine these very goals through misguided ideas of "helping" left-handed students adjust to a right-handed world? There is only one course of appropriate action—the right choice is clearly left.

Write About it

 Take two samples of your own writing, and review the conclusions you wrote. Revise them using what you have learned about effective concluding paragraphs.

  Check Your Writing Exchange papers with a partner. Use the questions below to give feedback to your partner. When you get your own paper back, revise as necessary.

- Are the main ideas clearly summarized?
- Is the ending memorable?

NOT!

YOU'RE NOT MY TYPE

GETTING STARTED

Warm Up

Even though each person's character is unique, psychologists claim that people share enough similarities to group them into personality types. People have been classified as thinkers or feelers, introverts or extroverts, or even according to their food preferences, their favorite seasons, or their blood types.

1. Work in small groups. Write three adjectives that describe your personality and that of the others in your group. Compare your answers. Does your view of yourself agree with the perceptions others have of you?

2. Listen to Mari and Phillip discussing their new neighbor. How does Mari describe their neighbor? How does Phillip describe him? What is a possible explanation for their different impressions?

Figure It Out

3. Fill out the personality questionnaire on the next page. Circle one answer for each question.

Are You a Feeler or a Thinker?

1. Which of the following best describes you?
   a. Hardworking and ambitious
   b. Talented and passionate
   c. Easy going and sociable

2. What do you do when you run into a problem?
   a. Go with whatever feels right
   b. Go over the facts and come to a solution
   c. Talk to a friend and make a decision

3. How do you react to new ideas?
   a. Compare them to other ideas
   b. Analyze them carefully
   c. Look at how they make you feel

4. How do your friends and family see you?
   a. As a person who is sensible and practical
   b. As a person who is a dreamer, impractical
   c. As a person who is funny and fun to be around

5. Which of the following do you enjoy most?
   a. Reading books, plays, or poems
   b. Painting and drawing
   c. Putting on plays or performing music for others

6. How do you respond when several things need to be done at the same time?
   a. Do the difficult ones first
   b. Do a part of each task
   c. Do the easy ones first

7. How do you feel about video games?
   a. They're easier to play than computer games.
   b. They're more fun than board games like chess.
   c. They're childish.

8. How would classmates or coworkers describe you?
   a. Unable to make up your mind
   b. Always in control
   c. Strong-willed and stubborn

9. How do you feel about instructions?
   a. They should always be carried out; they're there for a reason.
   b. They can be ignored; you can figure things out yourself.
   c. They are good guidelines but needn't be kept to strictly.

10. How do you tend to react when you first meet people?
   a. By opening up to them
   b. By holding back until you know them better
   c. By trying to make a good impression

Use the grid to calculate your total score.   Total score:____

Answer	Question Number									
	1	2	3	4	5	6	7	8	9	10
a.	10	4	7	10	7	10	4	7	10	4
b.	7	10	10	4	4	7	7	10	4	10
c.	4	7	4	7	10	4	10	4	7	7

Explanation of Score:

0-59 points: You are a feeler. You use your heart and intuition to make up your mind. Your thinking style is spatial, random, creative, and subjective. You don't like setting up plans because you feel that might cut down on your options.

60-80 points: You are a well-adjusted person who shares characteristics of both feelers and thinkers. You get along with others, but you never hold back your thoughts or feelings. Your thinking style is both spatial and well-structured. Because you are both logical and creative, you are excellent at figuring out solutions to problems.

81 points or higher: You are a thinker. You like to check up on details and look into things before acting. Your thinking style is verbal, orderly, and objective. You are articulate and social. You thrive in situations with a clear structure.

Vocabulary Check Match the words on the left with their meanings on the right.

_____ **1.** go with an idea (line 8)

_____ **2.** put on a show (lines 29-30)

_____ **3.** make up your mind (line 45)

_____ **4.** carry out plans (line 49)

_____ **5.** open up to someone (line 57)

_____ **6.** hold back information (lines 58-59)

a. stage a play for an audience

b. decide to do

c. do something you've been told to do

d. control yourself from saying or doing something

e. imagine or picture

f. come to a decision

g. speak about something freely

Talk About It

5 A counselor is explaining a personality test to a client. Work with a partner. Take turns being the counselor and the client, and discuss the character evaluation methods below. Use the conversation as a model.

Example: judge personality from handwriting analysis

ROLES	MODEL CONVERSATION	FUNCTIONS
Client:	So, what does my handwriting say about me?	Ask about results.
Counselor:	Well, from this sample, I'd say you're enthusiastic, energetic, and innovative. Do you agree?	Give a brief description of the results.
Client:	Well, I'd agree with enthusiastic and energetic, but not the innovative part.	Respond and give an opinion.
Counselor:	So what makes you say that?	Ask for an explanation.
Client:	I'm always stuck for new ideas when I have to do an assignment!	Respond.

<u>Character Evaluation Methods</u>

a. judge personality by color preferences

b. judge personality by pet preferences

c. judge personality based on birth order

d. judge personality by food preferences

e. (your own idea)

GRAMMAR

Phrasal Verbs

Phrasal verbs consist of a verb + particle (*look up a word*) or a verb + particle + preposition (*put up with noise*). Their meanings are different from the meanings of the separate parts of the phrasal verb. Phrasal verbs are common in English. Unlike phrasal verbs, some verbs are simply followed by a preposition before a complement. These verbs have no special meaning.

TWO-WORD PHRASAL VERBS

Verb	+	Particle	=	Meaning
Call		up (my mom)		telephone
Call		on (a friend)		visit
Put		off (an event)		delay
Get		over (an illness)		recover from
Turn		down (a job)		reject
Turn		up (at a place)		appear

THREE-WORD PHRASAL VERBS

Verb	+	Particle	+	Preposition	=	Meaning
Look		up		to (your father)		admire
Look		down		on (a relative)		feel a lack of respect for
Put		up		with (the noise)		tolerate
Get		rid		of (old clothes)		remove

Verb + Preposition

Look at (the cat)

Laugh at (the comic)

Stare at (the man)

Look for (the key)

Ask for (the check)

Listen to (music)

1 Underline the phrasal verbs in the questionnaire on page 96. Circle the verb + preposition combinations. Compare your answers with a partner's.

2 Read the article on the next page. Use the phrasal verbs in the box to complete the conversation that follows the article.

A common icebreaker at parties in the West is "What's your astrological sign?" The equivalent in Japan is "What's your blood type?" A recent survey indicated that as many as 75 percent of Japanese people believe that there is a connection between blood type and personality. The things you love, your strengths and weaknesses, the people you admire—all these can be determined by your blood type. Nearly every Japanese person knows his or her own blood type, and also which blood types are compatible with their own. The "blood type personalities" are:

- **Type A:** A's are cautious, loyal introverts. They are cooperative, conformist, and *enjoy being with people.*
- **Type B:** B personalities are cheerful, adventurous egocentrics. They are individualistic go-getters who can *appear* cold and inflexible but are good at *generating* new ideas and business.
- **Type AB:** AB's are the rarest type, *composed* of instinctive, easygoing diplomats. They have adaptability and charisma, but they also have a tendency to be troubled.
- **Type O:** Sociable, dramatic over-achievers, O's can also be opportunistic survivors who will *sacrifice* anything for success.

pointed out	give up	get along with	coming up with
figured out	look up to	come across as	made up of

WIFE: Honey, have you ever heard of the theory that there's a connection between personality and blood type?

HUSBAND: No, I can't say I have. Interesting!

WIFE: Well, a study **(1.)** _____ that at least 75 percent of Japanese believe blood type determines personalities. Someone's blood type decides who they **(2.)** _____, who they would hire for a job, and who they can marry.

HUSBAND: It's amazing to think that everything about your personality can be **(3.)** _____ from your blood type. What does it say about my blood type?

WIFE: You're an A, right? It says that you're cooperative, conformist, and that you **(4.)** _____ others. I guess that's you.

HUSBAND: Yeah, I'd go along with that. And what about you?

WIFE: The article said that type B's can **(5.)** _____ cold and inflexible. But we are good at **(6.)** _____ new ideas.

HUSBAND: And what's Bill's personality type?

WIFE: The AB group is **(7.)** _____ adaptable and charismatic individuals. That's our son all right!

HUSBAND: Absolutely! And what about his wife? Katie's an O.

WIFE: They are the overachievers. They'd **(8.)** _____ anything for success.

HUSBAND: That's so interesting! She's just like that! Not my type, but as long as Bill loves her.

Separable and Inseparable Phrasal Verbs

Phrasal verbs can be separable or inseparable. With inseparable phrasal verbs, there is only one word order. Nouns and pronouns always follow the preposition.

> **Inseparable Phrasal Verbs**
>
> Laura's the kind of person who **checks up on** <u>her boyfriend</u> every time he goes somewhere. She's so jealous, she even **checked up on** <u>him</u> when he went to the hospital to see his mother after her operation.

With separable phrasal verbs, the verb and particle can be separated. Noun objects can go either after the particle or between the verb and the particle. If the complement is a pronoun, it *must* go between the verb and the particle.

> **Separable Phrasal Verbs**
>
> My friend Ricky is always **turning down** <u>new experiences</u>. For example, he had a chance to play the lead in the school play, and he **turned** <u>it</u> **down**.

3 Circle the answer that correctly completes each sentence.

1. I am a little bit upset at my friend Maggie. She never calls me and behaves as if I don't exist, but as soon as she has a problem, she is sure to call _____ and ask for help.

   a. up me   **b.** me up

2. My colleague Rob is very accommodating and helpful. People sometimes take advantage of him, but he puts _____.

   a. up with it   **b.** it up with

3. Jack is the kind of person who loves to work. It's difficult to keep _____.

   a. up with his energy   **b.** his energy up with

4. My mother is such a pack rat. She has all her high-school notebooks and won't throw _____.

   a. away them   **b.** them away

5. My roommate Peggy is really outgoing and has met a lot of people since she moved to New York. She runs _____ wherever she goes.

   a. them into   **b.** into them

6. My friend Alex is a world traveler. I always love to hear _____ after a trip.

   a. from him   **b.** him from

4 Check Your Understanding Circle the boldface words that best complete the sentences. Compare your answers with a partner's.

In the past, the shape of the face was used to figure (**1. in/out**) someone's personality. People with long faces supposedly make strong leaders and organizers, and they are constantly going (**2. for/on**) excitement. They want results quickly, love to be the center of attention, and go (**3. along with/up for**) any idea that's fun. Short-faced people are practical and careful with money. They are advocates of planning and can't put (**4. up with/down on**) disorganization. When they come (**5. up with/down with**) a plan, they stick (**6. it to/to it**). They are methodical fact finders who can work (**7. out/up**) any problem. People with oval faces have good senses of humor and are hardworking. They get (**8. along for/along with**) everybody. Finally, the round face characterizes people who keep (**9. away/to**) themselves and are gentle and quiet. They're also always ready to help those in need and will make peace at any price.

  5 Express Yourself Write a paragraph describing yourself. Do not write your name on your paper. Pass in your paper and take another student's paper. Try to guess whose description you have.

LISTENING and SPEAKING

Listen: All in the Family

 Before You Listen Were you the oldest, middle, or youngest child in your family? Were you an only child? Do you feel this has made a difference in your personality? Does birth order determine a person's personality?

 Relating Information When listening for personal interpretation, effective listeners focus on the main ideas and key details that will help them relate the information they hear to their own lives.

  Listen to a conversation about a book review and circle the letter of the correct answer.

1. The people are talking about . . .
    a. how birth order affects financial prospects.
    b. how the oldest child has all the advantages.
    c. the order in which they were born in their families.

2. According to the book they are looking at, people's personalities . . .
    a. are shaped by their older siblings.
    b. can be influenced by their birth order.
    c. depend on the size of people's families.

3 Listen again and fill in the chart.

Person	Birth Order	Personality Characteristics	Accurate Description
Mark's brother	first child	strong sense of duty, demanding	yes
Jeanne			
Mark			
Charles			

4 What were some of the characteristics mentioned that correspond to your birth order? In your opinion, are they accurate descriptions of your personality?

Pronunciation

Two- and three-word verb combinations have different stress patterns.
In all of the patterns, the verb has at least one stressed syllable. Prepositions are usually not stressed but particles usually are. Noun complements are stressed; pronoun complements are not.

Verb	Preposition	Object	Verb	Object	Particle	Verb	Particle	Preposition	Object
talk	about	**love**	**call**	him	**up**	**run**	**out**	of	money
ask	for	**money**	**turn**	it	**down**	**check**	**up**	on	him
listen	to	**music**	**put**	it	**off**	**put**	**up**	with	her

5 Predict the stressed elements of the following two- and three-word verbs and underline them.

a. figure it out
b. disapprove of him
c. walk away from the job
d. look up to her

e. put off work
f. break out of jail
g. work out a deal
h. go for it

i. throw it away
j. get along with her
k. give it back
l. count on them

 6 Listen to check your predictions.

7 Work with a partner. Take turns saying the words aloud, focusing on stress patterns.

Speak Out

 Having the Floor The leader of a successful discussion makes sure that all participants take turns so that everyone has a chance to speak, or "has the floor." Usually a speaker gives up the floor willingly and allows another person to talk. Occasionally, a speaker may need to finish an important point and so refuses to give up the floor for a time. This behavior is usually considered impolite.

8 Decide if these expressions are **T** (turn taking), **G** (giving up the floor), or **R** (refusing to give up the floor).

__T__ **1.** I believe it's Pat's turn at the wheel.

_____ **2.** If you would just let me finish this up. . .

_____ **3.** How about five more minutes?

_____ **4.** What I have to say can wait. Be my guest.

_____ **5.** I'm afraid I really need to get a decision on this now.

_____ **6.** Is everyone OK if I pass? Then Luis can continue.

_____ **7.** Derek, we haven't heard what you think. So?

9 Work in groups of three. Read the situation below and take turns acting out the roles.

SITUATION:	Ken, Pat, and Carolina are discussing their research for their class project on color and personality.

ROLE A:	Ken is the group leader. It is his responsibility to make sure that everyone contributes.
ROLE B:	Carolina is a very opinionated student who tries to monopolize the floor.
ROLE C:	Pat is a very shy student with good ideas, but who seldom contributes to the discussion.

READING and WRITING

Read About It

1 **Before You Read** Work in small groups, and think of at least three advantages and disadvantages of categorizing people according to personality type.

 Making Inferences Writers often provide information in an article without actually stating it. When reading for understanding, readers get this information by making inferences, or by making associations that are not stated directly. In other words, they "read between the lines."

2 Read the article on personality types on the next page. As you read, look for information that is implied but left unstated. What is the tone of the article? Is it serious, skeptical, or somewhere in between? What does the tone indicate about the author's attitude toward the subject?

Unit 8

Personality's Part and Parcel

By Paul Chance

"There are," he said, "two kinds of people: idea people and feeling people. I think you're an idea person."

My speech professor was trying to
5 cheer me up after one of the more humiliating experiences in a humiliating freshman year. He had this idea that people would become better public speakers if they first practiced
10 doing really silly things in front of a group. He had me stand before the class, one foot in front of the other, and rock back and forth while swinging my arms, ape fashion, and chanting:
15 "Aaahhooooo, aaahhoooo." I did it, but I did it with an embarrassed stiffness you might expect from Richard Nixon if you made him moon walk. Like I said, it was humiliating.
20 The prof's philosophical musings were intended to assure me. "You'll never make it as an actor," he was saying, "but you might make it in some more bookish occupation." I took
25 the personality assessment in stride and immediately began wondering (as befitted my bookish personality) whether the entire human population could be categorized by this, or any
30 other, two-legged dichotomy. Was it really true that there were only two kinds of people in the world?

I had problems with the "feeling and idea" pigeonholes right from the
35 start. I couldn't help wondering why, if I was an idea person, I was in danger of flunking out of college. Was it because my classes placed little emphasis on ideas? I did do better
40 in subsequent years, when the ideas became more plentiful and interesting than they had been in my freshman

speech class. But somehow, the idea-feeling theory of personality came
45 across to me as lacking predictability.

Another problem I ran into was that there were lots of competing theories about the two kinds of people in the world. One familiar idea is that
50 everybody is either an optimist or a pessimist. Optimists are sure that they'll never die, and that if they do die they'll wake up to the glory of heaven. Pessimists are sure that they won't live
55 much longer, and that if they wake up in heaven, they won't like it.

Another theory says that people are either realists or idealists. A realist is a person who knows which side of the
60 bread is buttered; an idealist has more important things to worry about. The consensus is that realists eat better than idealists.

Other folks divide the human race
65 into animal people and plant people. Animal people talk to their furry and feathered companions in melodious tones about everything from the price of cheese to American foreign policy,
70 as if the animals picked up every word that was said. Plant people look upon such displays as sentimental and silly, and they expound upon their views in great detail to their annual and
75 perennial friends.

In recent years we've heard a lot about Type A and Type B personalities. Type B people eat lunch at home or in a restaurant and take
80 their time about doing it. Type A people ram down a hot dog while running up an escalator. Type A people work harder at making money than Type B people, but they don't

85 know how to enjoy it. Type B people know how to enjoy money, but aren't sure it's worth the bother to get it.

Of course, the idea that everyone can be tagged with one or two labels 90 doesn't appeal to everybody. There are lots of psychologists, for example, who would argue that there aren't two kinds of people, or six, or eight or thirty-seven. There are as many kinds 95 of people as there are people. And each person may be different people at different times. Being a human being is a complicated business, these psychologists point out, and you 100 cannot arbitrarily squeeze everybody into one of two categories.

Despite these doubts, I think there is some merit to the idea that there are two kinds of people. In fact, I've come 105 up with my own theory. I propose that there are two kinds of people in the world: those who believe there are two kinds of people and those who don't.

I place myself in the second 110 category. How about you?

Reprinted with permission from PSYCHOLOGY TODAY MAGAZINE, Copyright ©1988 Sussex Publishers, Inc.

3 Check the statements below that can be inferred from the article. Then compare your answers in small groups.

_____ **1.** The author is willing to try out new things.

_____ **2.** The author doesn't just accept answers but likes to come up with his own interpretations.

_____ **3.** The author had a smooth and easy start to college.

_____ **4.** The author takes the animal-plant people division seriously.

4 Discuss these questions in small groups.

a. Which personality categorizations does the author mention in the article?

b. What is the author's final assertion about personality types? Do you agree with it? Why or why not?

Think About It

5 Work with a partner. In general, which of the factors below influence your personality? Rank them from **1** (most important) to **9** (least important). Compare your rankings with your partner's. Then discuss the reasons for your ranking with another pair.

_____ heredity   _____ cultural values   _____ physical attractiveness

_____ gender   _____ life experiences   _____ social status

_____ intelligence   _____ parents' behavior   _____ (your own idea)

Write: Essays of Comparison and Contrast: Point-by-Point Organization

STRATEGY In an essay of comparison, similarities among two or more items are explored. In an essay of contrast, differences among two or more items are explored. One structural pattern used in support paragraphs for these essay types is that of point-by-point organization. In this type of organization, both items being compared or contrasted are treated together in each supporting paragraph. The first support paragraph examines one aspect of both items, the second support paragraph examines a second aspect of both items, and the third support paragraph examines a third aspect of both items.

In an essay comparing Western and Eastern astrology, for example, the following point-by-point organization could apply in the support paragraphs:

Support Paragraph 1:	use of relationships among stars and planets
	(a) in Western astrology
	(b) in Eastern astrology
Support Paragraph 2:	use of symbols from the natural world to divide temporal periods
	(a) in Western astrology
	(b) in Eastern astrology
Support Paragraph 3:	personality types determined by time of birth and position of stars, planets
	(a) in Western astrology
	(b) in Eastern astrology

6 **Write About It** Write an essay comparing the personality of a family member or friend with your own.

7 **Check Your Writing** Exchange papers with a partner. Use the questions below to give feedback to your partner. When you get your own paper back, revise as necessary.

- Is there a clear introduction with a thesis statement?
- Are the supporting paragraphs organized in a clear point-by-point sequence?
- Is there a clear conclusion?

GETTING STARTED

Warm Up

Unlike the TV, the computer has gone through radical changes from its original form. Will this trend continue?

1 Think of technologies that are widely used today that didn't exist when you were a child. Compare lists in small groups. Discuss technologies that existed when you were a child.

2 What technologies might replace today's? Brainstorm ideas with your group.

3 Bill Gates, a founder of Microsoft, is the richest man in North America. Work with a partner. Before you listen, predict what is unusual about the technologies he has in his home, and fill in the chart. Then listen to check your predictions.

	Your Prediction	**The Reality**
TV		
Bath		
Sound System		
Garage Security System		

Figure It Out!

Computer ethics refers to following moral guidelines for computer use. Software piracy and the unauthorized selling of personal information are obviously unethical. Other situations are less clear-cut.

4 Decide if the actions below are ethical or unethical. Then compare your anwers with a partner's.

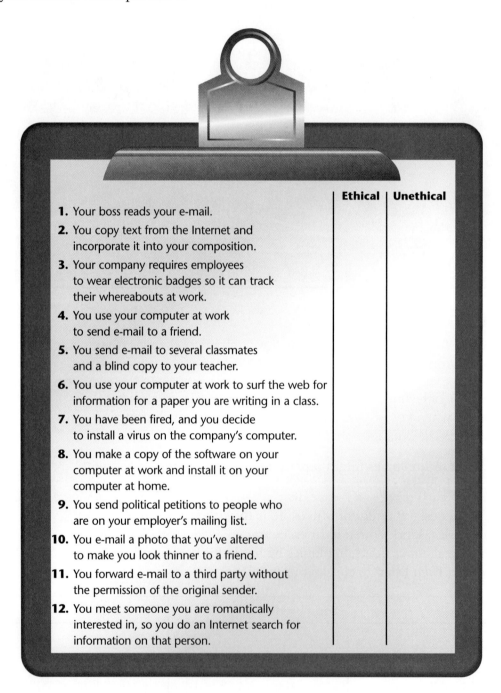

	Ethical	Unethical
1. Your boss reads your e-mail.		
2. You copy text from the Internet and incorporate it into your composition.		
3. Your company requires employees to wear electronic badges so it can track their whereabouts at work.		
4. You use your computer at work to send e-mail to a friend.		
5. You send e-mail to several classmates and a blind copy to your teacher.		
6. You use your computer at work to surf the web for information for a paper you are writing in a class.		
7. You have been fired, and you decide to install a virus on the company's computer.		
8. You make a copy of the software on your computer at work and install it on your computer at home.		
9. You send political petitions to people who are on your employer's mailing list.		
10. You e-mail a photo that you've altered to make you look thinner to a friend.		
11. You forward e-mail to a third party without the permission of the original sender.		
12. You meet someone you are romantically interested in, so you do an Internet search for information on that person.		

Talk About It

A customer in a computer store is talking to the sales clerk. Work with a partner. Take turns being the customer and the sales clerk, and discuss the products below. Use the conversation as a model.

Example: a laptop computer

ROLES	MODEL CONVERSATION	FUNCTIONS
Customer:	I'm in the market for a laptop computer.	State a need.
Sales Clerk:	I see. And exactly what features are you looking for?	Respond and ask for specifics.
Customer:	Well, I need something that's really fast because I spend a lot of time on the Web.	Specify the need.
Sales Clerk:	Well, our really fast models are over here. But, in general, really fast laptops with the latest processors are expensive.	Provide general information about the product.

Products

a. MP3 player

b. cable modem

c. virus protection program

d. DVD player

e. digital camera

f. (your own idea)

GRAMMAR

Nouns and Articles

Nouns that can be counted (computers, mouse pads) are called count nouns. Nouns referring to things that cannot be divided or counted (computer memory, progress) are called non-count nouns. Count nouns are either singular or plural, whereas non-count nouns cannot have a plural.

Specific Reference: The Definite Article

When talking about a specific person, place, or thing, we use the **definite article (the)**. Definite articles are used with count and non-count nouns.

> **A:** Have we hooked up **the scanner** yet? (we know which scanner)
>
> **B:** No, it's still in one of **the boxes**. (we know which boxes)

Non-Specific Reference: Indefinite Articles

To refer to a non-specific person, place, or thing, we use an **indefinite article** *(a/an)*. We use *a/an* with singular count nouns (a machine = "any machine" or "one of many" machines). We do not use an article with plural count nouns (Ø machines = "several" or "a few" machines) or with non-count nouns (Ø progress = "any amount of" or "some" progress).

> **A:** Does the company have **a scanner**?
>
> **B:** Yeah, there are **scanners** in the lab.

Generic Reference: Definite and Indefinite Articles

When we are talking generally about persons, places, or things (generic reference), we usually use plural nouns, and therefore **no** article (cameras are fun.) We can also use an indefinite or definite article with a singular count noun for generic reference.

 1 Work with a partner. Complete the chart by writing example sentences on a separate sheet of paper. Ø = no article

	Specific Reference	Non-Specific Reference	Generic Reference
Singular Count Nouns	I want **the** camera.	I want **a** camera. I want **an** MP3 player.	**The** camera is a great invention. **A** telephone is important. **An** MP3 player is amazing.
Plural Count Nouns	I bought **the** cameras.	I shopped for Ø cameras.	Ø Cameras are fun.
Non-Count Nouns	I see **the** progress.	I see Ø progress.	Ø Progress is important.

2 Work with a partner. Read each sentence and check the statement below it that best describes it.

  a. You should install a virus protection program.
  - [ ] One of many virus protection programs should be installed.
  - [ ] A specific virus protection program should be installed.

  b. What if I have sensitive information on my computer?
  - [ ] The question is about specific sensitive information.
  - [ ] The question is about any sensitive information.

  c. Open e-mail attachments only if you know and trust the sender.
  - [ ] You should accept attachments from only one specific sender.
  - [ ] You should accept attachments from any sender you trust.

d. Start a "dummy" e-mail account from a free provider for shopping and web surfing.

☐ There is more than one free provider you can start an account with.

☐ There is only one free provider you can start an account with.

e. Check privacy policies of websites you visit.

☐ You should check the policies of specific websites.

☐ You should check the policies of all websites.

f. Encryption can always be cracked.

☐ All encryption can be figured out.

☐ Only specific kinds of encryption can be figured out.

3 Read the following article. Complete the sentences with *a*, *an*, *the*, or Ø.

Disposable Phones

One day **(1.)** _____ Randi was driving down **(2.)** _____ highway talking on her cellular phone. Suddenly, **(3.)** _____ signal disappeared and she lost her connection. It was **(4.)** _____ very important conversation, and the fact that she couldn't finish it made her so angry that she wanted to throw **(5.)** _____ phone out **(6.)** _____ window. The only thing that stopped her was that the phone was too expensive. That's when the idea struck her: there should be **(7.)** _____ cell phone so inexpensive that **(8.)** _____ people wouldn't have to worry about losing it or breaking it. If that were possible, you could keep one in your car, carry one with you, and give one to every member of your family. Later, with the help of **(9.)** _____ team of engineers, she found **(10.)** _____ way to do this: make the phone out of **(11.)** _____ paper!

This new phone has its circuitry printed on paper with **(12.)** _____ magnetic ink. **(13.)** _____ lengthy, flexible circuit on the paper will then be folded accordion-like to form **(14.)** _____ body of the phone. The current version of the prototype contains two traditional silicon chips, but by the third generation, the new phone will have no **(15.)** _____ chips in it.

The paper phone is about the size of **(16.)** _____ credit card, and it can easily fit in a wallet. There is an earpiece and a tiny microphone attached to it, guaranteeing excellent audio quality. **(17.)** _____ whole device will cost about ten dollars and will come with sixty minutes of airtime. When **(18.)** _____ sixty minutes expire, you can throw it away or add more **(19.)** _____ time with the push of **(20.)** _____ button.

While this phone is in itself **(21.)** _____ very important discovery which will radically change **(22.)** _____ telecommunications industry, its impact may be far greater than that. It could revolutionize the whole electronics industry! If the printed circuitry works out and can be transferred to other devices—which is very likely—every electronic device will be able to work without **(23.)** _____ circuit board and **(24.)** _____ silicon chips. And that's as close as it gets to a revolution in **(25.)** _____ industry! ∎

4 **Check Your Understanding** Write definitions like the examples.

Examples: A clone is _an exact copy of a plant or animal._

Videophones are _telephones with videoscreens._

a. Science is _____

b. A solar-powered house has _____

c. Robots _____

d. An MP3 player _____

 5 **Express Yourself** Work with a partner. Take turns reading aloud your sentences from the exercise above. Ask and answer questions about them.

 LISTENING and SPEAKING

Listen: Tech Pets

1 **Before You Listen** Do you have a pet at home? If so, what kind? What is its name? What are the pleasures and the responsibilities of having a pet?

STRATEGY **Identifying Implications** When listening for critical analysis, effective listeners focus on pertinent information that will help them form opinions and make decisions. They identify the criteria that will determine the long-term and short-term implications, or consequences of an action.

 2 Listen to the conversation about tech pets. Summarize the main ideas in a sentence or two.

3 Listen again and note information that would help you make a decision about owning a tech pet or buying one as a gift.

Muy Loco	I-Cybie
Features:	Features:
Target Age:	Target Age:
Price:	Price:

Pronunciation

In casual speech, we sometimes stress words that we normally would not stress in order to confirm that we have heard or have understood something correctly. For example, if we didn't hear something very well, we can use sentence stress to ask about the word we are clarifying.

Confirming Stress

A: I'm sorry, what did you say your **favorite** technological invention was?

B: I said the **digital camera** was.

 Work with a partner. Predict which words should receive confirming stress and underline them.

1. A: You said those tiny robots were called microbots?

   B: No, they are called nanobots.

2. A: Eighty percent of the people in a recent poll said they prefer hydrogen as a fuel as opposed to gas?

   B: No, eighteen percent!

3. A: Hey, look at this! It's a toothbrush that warns you of an imminent heart attack!

   B: A toothbrush can warn you a heart attack's coming?

   A: Yep, so they say. Incredible!

4. A: Did you say you had a problem with your ROM?

   B: No, I said RAM!

  Listen to the conversations to check your predictions.

 Work with a partner. Take turns reading the dialogues, focusing on confirming stress.

Speak Out

 Managing Disruptive Behavior Usually, the purpose of discussions and meetings is problem solving and decision making. Sometimes, participants lose sight of this goal and indulge in behavior that blocks the progress of the group (blocking behaviors). They may waste the group's time by joking too much, focusing attention on themselves, displaying impatience or anger, bringing up irrelevant topics, refusing to participate in the discussion, or dominating the discussion. It is the responsibility of all group members to politely discourage these kinds of disruptive behaviors (managing blocking behaviors).

 Read the exchange between Jeff and Anne. How does Anne let Jeff know that he is blocking the group's progress?

JEFF: Anyway, what you just said reminds me of another joke. Did you hear the one about . . .

ANNE: You're really funny, Jeff, but you'll have to save the jokes until we've finished our work. It will be something to look forward to!

8 The following statements are either **B** (blocking behaviors) or **M** (managing blocking behaviors). Write **B** or **M** on the line.

_____ **a.** I believe we've already discussed that. Let's all pay attention.

_____ **b.** Anyway, there's the greatest sale going on downtown. I read all the ads and cut the coupons out from today's paper.

_____ **c.** Marge, we really can't wait for you to go through your entire file cabinet to find what you're looking for right now. I'll help you later, if you like.

_____ **d.** That's a great story, Phil, but you'll have to wait until the meeting is over to tell us the rest. Sorry.

_____ **e.** Vera, we appreciate your intense interest, but it's time to let others express their views on the subject.

_____ **f.** So in the last ten seconds of the game, he scores! And then the sports announcer said that he had broken the record!

_____ **g.** I appreciate your concern, but this is Frank's decision to make, not yours. Let's let him do his job.

9 Work in groups. Discuss trends in technology that interest you. Take turns engaging in blocking behaviors and in managing those behaviors during your discussion.

READING and WRITING

Read About It

1 **Before You Read** With recent advances in genetic engineering, it might soon be possible to change eye and hair color, intelligence, and even personality. If this technology were available today, would you choose to enhance either your appearance or your intelligence? Discuss your answers in small groups.

STRATEGY ➤ **Assessing Function** When reading critically, effective readers try to assess both the purpose and function of a text. The way the text is written may cause it to function quite differently from its declared purpose. Is the author using language to persuade us, warn us, or raise our awareness? Is the author protesting against something, trying to give advice, or simply giving information? There can be multiple purposes or functions in the same text.

Read the selection. As you read, note how the author presents information. Is the function of the text clear?

Enhanced Intelligence: *A Smart Idea?*

We are not far from an era when it will be possible to choose the physical traits of children to be born. With some
5 in-utero gene manipulation, you will soon be able to customize your child according to your tastes. You might be able to choose skin, eye, and hair color, the shape of the nose and lips,
10 body height and build. Appealing as this may sound, such a procedure might put in danger one of the most precious characteristics of humanity: its variety. In the rush to look
15 beautiful, people will all start looking similar: taller and slimmer. For people who cherish variety, this is a frightening thought.

Here's an even more intriguing
20 question: If you could choose not just your children's appearance, but make them smarter through genetic engineering, would you do it? The first impulse of most of us would be
25 to say "Absolutely!" Who wouldn't want to have a smarter child? They get into better schools and colleges, have better jobs, and make more money. However, genetic engineering
30 is not without risk. It will have permanent, long-lasting effects. What if something goes wrong? What if there are unwanted side effects? Specialists say that if you
35 make a change in one area of the human organism, it may bring about subtle changes in other areas. It may lead to a change in the child's personality, for instance. He or she

40 will be smarter but more selfish, or wittier but very shy. Would you still want to choose to have this done, keeping these risks in mind? Would you say "no" even if
45 everybody else around you opted for genetic enhancement?

These are very tough questions, and for now they are only theoretical. But with the human genome
50 decoded, an IQ gene supposedly discovered, and all the focus on cutting-edge biotechnology research, these theoretical questions can become real issues very soon.

55 We are already on a slippery slope with procedures originally intended only to cure but consequently used to enhance, such as the use of human growth hormones. Human
60 growth hormones were intended for children with serious growth deficiencies, but they've come to be used on healthy children who are just unhappy with their short stature.
65 (If their parents can afford up to $30,000 a year for injections, that is.) Prenatal sex-selection tests were developed to weed out diseases that affect one gender or the other, such
70 as hemophilia. However, these tests are now being used to allow parents to select the gender of their future children. In the same manner, if doctors can someday manipulate
75 genes to treat children with autism, for example, what is to stop them from genetically changing a child's personality or intelligence?

(continued on next page)

Besides the problem of
80 undesirable side effects due to
gene manipulation, there is also
the issue of fairness. When such
enhancements are available,
they will most certainly come
85 with exorbitant fees. Every
parent in the world would want
them, of course, but only those
who can afford such treatments
will get them. Will genetic
90 enhancement create a new form
of discrimination against
"normal," unenhanced children,
with lower IQs? How will this
technology affect choosing one's
95 marriage partner? Or applying

for a job? Furthermore, who will
have the right to know whether
a person is naturally smart or
has had an artificial boost?
100 Before we start analyzing these
issues, we need to ask a more
fundamental question: Why would
we want to enhance intelligence
in the first place? Will it make
105 us happier? We have all seen
very smart but unhappy people.
Will it make us rich? Possibly,
but there are no guarantees. If
ignorance is indeed bliss, then
110 perhaps enhanced intelligence
is a foolhardy notion.

 Work with a partner and answer the questions. Then compare your
answers with another pair's.

  a. What is the function of the passage? What helped you decide?

  b. What advantages and disadvantages of intellectual enhancement
are presented?

  c. What present-day medical practices are mentioned in the text?
What point is made through these examples?

  d. How can intellectual enhancement lead to discrimination?

  e. Does an enhanced memory mean a happier person? Explain.

  Vocabulary Check Use the context to determine the meaning of
these words. Write short definitions in your notebook. Compare your
definitions with a partner's.

  a. trait (line 3)   **f.** subtle (line 37)

  b. customize (line 6)   **g.** enhancement (line 46)

  c. appealing (line 10)   **h.** cutting-edge (line 52)

  d. intriguing (line 19)   **i.** weed out (line 68)

  e. side effect (lines 33-34)

Think About It

 Do you think that genetically enhanced humans will be part
of our future? Why or why not?

Write: Essay of Comparison

As you learned in Unit 8, an essay of comparison or contrast may be organized in point-by-point style. In the body of the essay, the first support paragraph discusses the first point of similarity or difference for both items, the second paragraph the second point of similarity or difference for both items, and the third paragraph the third point of similarity or difference for both items.

In an essay comparing robotic pets and real pets, for example, sequential organization in the body of the essay could include the following information:

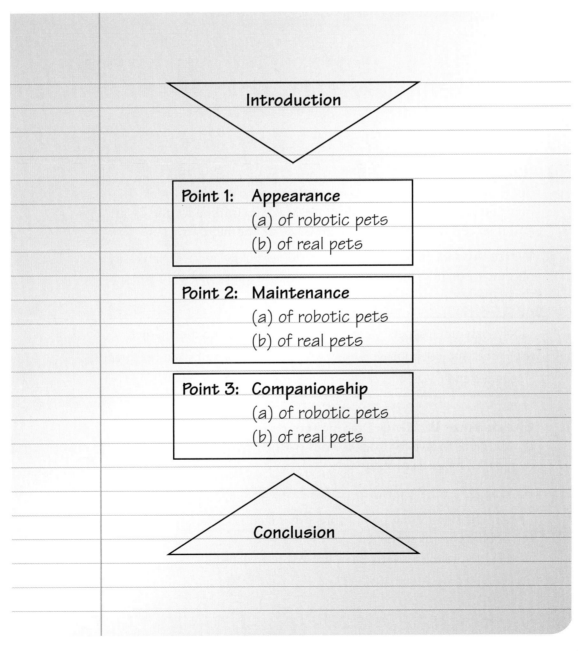

Introduction

Point 1: Appearance
   (a) of robotic pets
   (b) of real pets

Point 2: Maintenance
   (a) of robotic pets
   (b) of real pets

Point 3: Companionship
   (a) of robotic pets
   (b) of real pets

Conclusion

STRATEGY When composing an essay of comparison, effective writers use transition words and expressions to show how the items under discussion are alike.

alike	both	like	much as
as	in the same way	likewise	similarly

Examples:

Both the computer and the telephone have changed substantially since their first prototypes.

Hand-held computers allow you to send and receive e-mail when you are away from your computer. **Similarly,** cell phones allow you to write, send, and read messages from a remote location.

6 Work with a partner. Brainstorm points you would include in a point-by-point essay of comparison discussing the similarities between typewriters and computers. Make an outline for the essay, and then compare your ideas with those of another pair.

7 **Write About It** Choose one of the topics below and write an essay of comparison in sequential style. Be sure to use appropriate transitions of comparison.

robotic pets and real pets	books and the Internet
telephones and cell phones	photographs and holographs
videotapes and DVDs	(your own idea)

 8 **Check Your Writing** Exchange your paper with a partner. Use the questions to give feedback to your partner. When you receive your own paper, revise as necessary.

- Is there a clear introduction with a thesis statement?
- Are the supporting paragraphs organized in a clear point-by-point sequence?
- Have transition words been used appropriately?
- Is there a clear conclusion?

GRAMMAR

A Circle the letter of the best answer to complete each sentence.

1. Although no one knows for sure what causes left-handedness, researchers have _____ with various theories.   A B Ⓒ D
   (A) come in   **(C)** come up
   (B) come on   **(D)** come about

2. One of the less popular theories is an environmental theory _____ main support is the positioning of ancient warriors' swords and shields.   A B C D
   (A) that   **(C)** where
   (B) whose   **(D)** which

3. Warriors held their swords in their right hands and their shields in their left hands in order to better protect their hearts. The theory claims that because _____ warriors were less likely to survive the battle, right-handedness became the norm.   A B C D
   (A) left-handed   **(C)** the left-handed
   (B) a left-handed   **(D)** any left-handed

4. This theory does not hold up for many reasons, _____ being that it doesn't explain why right-handedness would be more prevalent among women than men.   A B C D
   (A) main one   **(C)** main ones
   (B) a main one   **(D)** the main one

5. Today, scientists are willing to _____ these environmental theories because despite the same environment, handedness is not uniform in siblings.   A B C D
   (A) throw in   **(C)** throw out
   (B) throw up   **(D)** throw around

6. Developmental theories, _____ often refer to both genetic and environmental influences, have an advantage over many other theories because they don't rely on only one or the other.   A B C D
   (A) who   **(C)** whom
   (B) that   **(D)** which

7. In addition, they help to account for the fact that right or left brain   **A B C D**
hemispheric dominance is already established at _____.
  (A) birth   **(C)** a birth
  (B) births   **(D)** the birth

8. The best-known developmental theory was established by the   **A B C D**
Geschwind-Galaburda team _____ claim that high levels of
testosterone affect the growth of the left hemisphere of the brain,
causing right-hemispheric dominance.
  (A) that   **(C)** who
  (B) which   **(D)** whose

> **STRATEGY**   **TIME MANAGEMENT ON TESTS** Before you take a standardized test, make sure you know how much time is allotted to each section. Watch your time very carefully. Do not spend too much time on any one item. If you find an item is too hard, skip over it, answer the items you know, and then go back and answer the more difficult items.

B   **Each item has four underlined words or phrases. One of these underlined words or phrases is incorrect. Circle the letter of the word or phrase that is incorrect**

1. Some believe that personality can be categorized into one of   **Ⓐ B C D**

  <u>the</u> four different temperaments. They believe if you know <u>which</u>
  A   **B**

  temperament you are, you can improve yourself and your relationships

  because you will better understand your own weaknesses and be in <u>a</u> better
                                                                C

  position to <u>put up with</u> the weaknesses of the people you associate with.
           D

2. One pop psychologist has developed <u>a</u> system of four temperaments   **A B C D**
                                                         A

  <u>which</u> uses <u>a</u> lion, beaver, otter, and golden retriever as examples of the
  B   **C**

  four types, one of which they say everyone's personality <u>falls out of</u>.
                                                   D

3. Personality typing is utilized by some schools and employers for <u>the</u>   **A B C D**
                                                               A

  information <u>that they believe</u> provides them with clues as to how
            B

  <u>a</u> prospective student or employee may <u>work it out</u>.
  C   **D**

4. However, using personality typing in <u>recruitment decisions</u> is
   A

   controversial, because it is not a perfect science <u>who</u> can be <u>counted on</u>
   B   C

   to reliably predict behavior and so can be used to judge <u>people</u> unfairly.
   D

   A B C D

5. Many prospective bosses judge people <u>whom they interview</u> by whether
   A

   or not they think <u>the interviewees</u> are Type A or Type B personality types,
   B

   <u>whose the interviewers believe</u> can be fairly easily <u>figured out</u>.
   C   D

   A B C D

6. <u>Type A people</u> are thought of as being easily angered but extremely
   A

   hard-working, energetic, and success-oriented while <u>Type B people</u>,
   B

   <u>who</u> are considered to be calmer, may be easier people to work with and
   C

   <u>get along</u>.
   D

   A B C D

VOCABULARY

GUESSING ON MULTIPLE CHOICE TESTS When you are unsure of the one best answer, cross out the ones you can eliminate. Then make a guess from the remaining choices. Be careful, as some tests count blank answers as wrong. In this case, it is better to guess. Other tests will penalize you for wrong answers to discourage guessing. Make sure you know the policy on guessing BEFORE you take a standardized test.

Circle the letter of the word(s) that comes closest in meaning to the boldface words in each sentence.

SECTION ONE

1. One of the problems of depending on personality typologies is that as people change personality traits **revealed** about a person today could be inaccurate in the future.
   (A) hides   (C) withholds
   (B) states   (D) discloses

   A B C D

2. A left-handed child forced to use her right hand by a misguided   **A B C D**
    teacher could easily begin to **dread** going to school altogether.
    (A) refuse   **(C)** be fearful of
    (B) object to   **(D)** have nightmares about

3. Buying something with a **faulty** part is not uncommon in this day   **A B C D**
    and age when manufacturers are attempting to produce as much as
    possible in as short a time as possible.
    (A) used   **(C)** dirty
    (B) spare   **(D)** defective

4. New technology is bringing **enhancements** to every part of our lives.   **A B C D**
    (A) resentments   **(C)** enlargements
    (B) inducements   **(D)** improvements

SECTION TWO

1. Some of the results of studies done on left-handedness and its   **A B C D**
    association with certain diseases are **disturbing**.
    (A) prompting disbelief   **(C)** producing false data
    (B) causing worry or fear   **(D)** motivating further research

2. A majority of people who have their own computers today do not   **A B C D**
    have computers which are on the **cutting edge**.
    (A) most useful for all needs   **(C)** most expensive
    (B) most basic and user-friendly   **(D)** most advanced stage
                                                     of development

3. Some people feel that people with Type B personalities make good   **A B C D**
    teachers because they tend to be more **accommodating** with
    needy students.
    (A) willing to help   **(C)** inclined to motivate
    (B) able to be patient   **(D)** capable of understanding

WRITING

STRATEGY ► **ANSWERING ESSAY QUESTIONS:** Many standardized tests require test takers to demonstrate
their ability to write an essay. Read the topic carefully and make a brief outline of how to
answer the question. Begin writing your answer. Be careful with time. Try to allow yourself
time to read over your essay to correct any errors in grammar, spelling, or punctuation.

• Some people believe that recent technological advances have created
   unresolved ethical and legal problems. Write an essay about a specific
   problem resulting from a recent technological advance. State your
   opinion, and use specific reasons and examples to support your position.

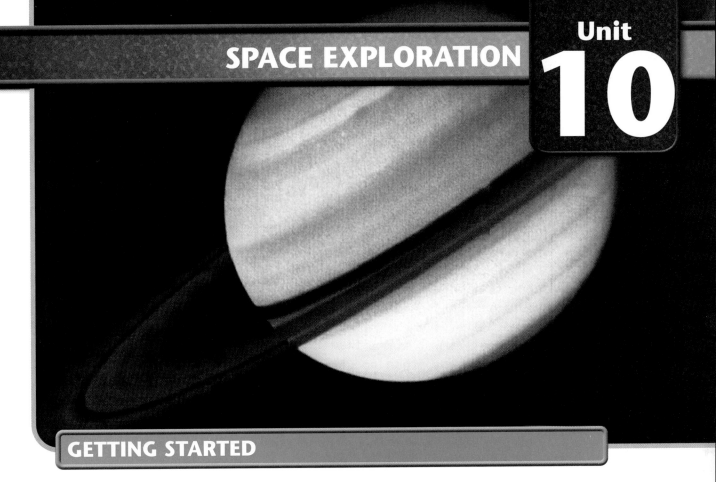

GETTING STARTED

Warm Up

The launch of *Sputnik* on October 4, 1957, began a revolution in human-kind's exploration of space. Since then, billions of dollars have been spent yearly on space exploration. What is the value of exploring outer space? What can we learn? What can we hope to attain?

1 Should humans travel in space? Choose the response that best describes your opinion, and share your answer with the class.

   a. We should invest our time and money on our home here on earth.

   b. We should reach for the stars—our future lies there.

   c. We should solve social problems such as poverty and war first—then go to space.

2 Listen to a news report. As you listen, answer the questions below.

   a. Who is the report about? _____

   b. Where is he/she going? _____

   c. What is unusual about this person? _____

   d. Why is he/she doing this? _____

Figure It Out

 John Laporte is a commentator for the radio program *Good Morning*. Read his interview with Sara Chang, a scientist from NASA, about space travel.

JOHN: Today in the studio, we have with us Sara Chang, one of the most prominent planetary scientists working for NASA. She'll be discussing the challenges facing future space tourists. Sara, what would you say is the most important thing future space tourists need to know?

5

SARA: Well, first of all, I think it's important to realize that just getting to space is a grueling experience because the force of gravity at takeoff is three times stronger than what we are used to on earth.

JOHN: Sounds daunting!

10 **SARA:** And that's not the end of it. Once they reach orbit, many would-be space travelers will be experiencing extreme motion sickness. This happens even with seasoned test pilots who've never been sick.

JOHN: Now I'm having second thoughts about one day going on a voyage to Mars! So, what else will space tourists be dealing with?

15 **SARA:** Weight loss.

JOHN: Well, sorry Sara, but that doesn't sound like a problem to me. I can imagine hundreds of people going into space instead of dieting.

SARA: But losing weight this way is a problem. Weight loss will occur because many of the body's organs will be going through major

20 changes.

JOHN: What do you mean exactly?

SARA: Well, the heart will become slightly enlarged, the legs will shrink, and the spinal discs will expand. And with no gravity to fight against, their muscles will soon be deteriorating.

25 **JOHN:** I guess if I want to step on Mars one day, I'd better hit the gym now, so my muscles can take it.

SARA: But it's not just the body that will be affected. The mind will be as well.

JOHN: I've also heard that the sun rises and sets sixteen times a day

30 in space. What effect does that have?

SARA: Space travelers don't sleep very well.

JOHN: I'm really shocked. The folks on *Star Trek* never had these problems.

SARA: (giggle) That's because Hollywood has spacy problems of its own.

35 **JOHN:** Seriously, all of these hardships on the human body sound so grim. I'm certainly glad that the first scheduled flight beyond the atmosphere won't be taking off for quite a while!

SARA: It's true, getting into space is no piece of cake. But I think it's also important to realize that you don't have to be superhuman to

40 adapt to space. What's more, I'm sure that by the end of this decade, commercial space tourism will have become commonplace.

JOHN: Thank you, Sara. I hope I live to see it.

Vocabulary Check Match the words on the left with their meanings on the right.

_____	**1.**	prominent (line 2)
_____	**2.**	grueling (line 7)
_____	**3.**	would-be (line 10)
_____	**4.**	seasoned (line 12)
_____	**5.**	have second thoughts (line 13)
_____	**6.**	commonplace (line 42)

a. routine, typical
b. doubt
c. experienced
d. difficult
e. well-known
f. weakening
g. prospective

Talk About It

5 A planetary scientist is discussing predictions about space travel with a radio talk show host. Work with a partner. Take turns being the scientist and the journalist, and discuss the situations below. Use the conversation as a model.

Example: manned flights to Mars

ROLES	MODEL CONVERSATION	FUNCTIONS
Scientist:	Well, I think by 2019, we'll be sending our first manned spacecraft to Mars.	State a prediction about a specific time in the future.
Host:	Oh, really? So soon?	Express surprise. Ask for confirmation.
Scientist:	I think so. By then we will have designed much faster spacecraft.	Confirm and elaborate about future accomplishments.
Host:	It's amazing how far space exploration has come!	Assess the situation.

Situations

a. space stations orbiting earth

b. time travel

c. colonization of other planets

d. contact with beings from outer space

e. manned flights to Saturn

f. (your own idea)

GRAMMAR

The Future Progressive Tense

We use the future progressive tense to talk about actions that will be in progress at a specified time in the future. The future progressive consists of a future form such as *will* or *be going to*, together with *be* + verb-*ing*. As with other progressive tenses, stative verbs (*have, believe, wish*) are usually not used in the future progressive. We use the future instead.

> At this time tomorrow, the first space tourist **will be taking** the shuttle to the International Space Station. He **will be spending** one week in space. While in space he **is going to be assisting** the astronauts at the Space Station with scientific experiments.

1 Go back to the conversation on page 124. Underline all the uses of future progressive tense. Compare your answers with a partner's.

2 Circle the italicized verb form that best completes each prediction.

1. **A:** Let's meet tomorrow to discuss the latest images we received of Jupiter.
   B: Could we make it next week? I'll *meet/I'll be meeting* with a group of visiting scientists from Mexico tomorrow.

2. **A:** In 2012, the moon *will become/will be becoming* an important power supply for the planet earth.
   B: That will be a major step in solving our energy crisis.

3. **A:** Could you hand me that advertisement on trips to Mars?
   B: I'll *get it/be getting it* for you in a second.

4. **A:** Hello, I'm calling to make a reservation to visit the Hubble telescope on March 21st.
   B: I'm sorry. All available observation slots are booked. We *won't take/ won't be taking* reservations for a while.

5. **A:** We *will need/will be needing* low-cost space shuttle launches within the next five years to make space tourism a reality.
   B: I think that's possible. Rocket engineers predict that before the year is over, we *will have/will be having* the necessary technology.

6. **A:** At this time tomorrow, I'm *going to be floating/going to float* in the International Space Station, enjoying the view of Earth!
   B: You're a lucky guy!

7. **A:** We *will probably send/will probably be sending* a person to Mars by the year 2019.
   B: That'll be a very challenging trip.

The Future Perfect Tense

We use the future perfect tense to express an action that will be completed before a specified point of time in the future. The future perfect tense is formed with *will* + *have* + past participle.

> Some researchers are now predicting that within thirty years, space travel **will have become** commonplace, and by the end of the 21st century, we **will have established** a settlement on Mars.

3 Look at the examples above. What are two time phrases commonly used with the future perfect tense?

_____

_____

4 Work with a partner. Read each sentence and decide if the statement following it has an **S** (similar meaning) or **D** (different one).

1. By 2010, the first space hotel will have been built.

_____ The first space hotel will be built sometime before 2010.

2. The space shuttle *Alpha* won't have arrived on Mars by this time next year.

_____ The space shuttle *Alpha* will be on Mars before next year.

3. By the time the first space hotel is built, the price of space travel will have gone down.

_____ The price of space travel will be cheaper once the first space hotel is built.

4. By this time next month, I will have visited the Lunar Hilton.

_____ I have already been to the Lunar Hilton.

5. By the next millennium, we will have found other intelligent life in the universe.

_____ We expect to find intelligent life in the universe sometime within the next millenium.

6. The space probe *Cassini* will have started orbiting Saturn within the next three years.

_____ *Cassini* will be orbiting Saturn three years from now.

5 Work with a partner. Take turns predicting what you both will have accomplished in the following areas ten years from now.

work	travel	home	finances
family	education	relationships	(your own idea)

6 **Check Your Understanding** Complete this ad for a trip to Raiza using the appropriate forms of the words in parentheses. Compare your answers with a partner's.

VISIT RAIZA

Do you need a break from your earthly troubles? We have the ultimate space experience for you! By this time next week you **(1. fly)** _____ at warp speed past Pluto on your way to Raiza, our amazing intergalactic resort. After Pluto, you **(2. travel)** _____ out of our galaxy into deep space. Raiza is another two days away. By the time you **(3. arrive)** _____ in Raiza, you **(4. learn)** _____ a few words of the language and been taught the local customs. At this time next winter, you **(5. enjoy)** _____ the Raizan beaches and waterfalls while friends back home **(6. deal)** _____ with the stresses of bad weather, traffic, and work. By the end of your stay in Raiza, you **(7. leave)** _____ your troubles behind and **(8. book)** _____ your next stay. Experience the thrills: Raiza.

  7 **Express Yourself** Write a paragraph on new frontiers we will be exploring ten years from now and what achievements will have occurred between then and now. Share your predictions in small groups.

Example: In ten years' time, planetary scientists will be preparing for the first colony on Mars. By then, they will have already resolved the problems which harm the human body in space.

LISTENING and SPEAKING

Listen: Where Is Planet X?

 1 **Before You Listen** Can you name the planets in our solar system in their order from the sun? Do you think there might be undiscovered planets in our own solar system? Why or why not?

Interpreting Relationships Between Ideas When listening
for understanding and personal interpretation, it is important to listen
for relationships, such as cause and effect, and the information needed to
draw conclusions and make predictions. This helps the listener discern
key ideas.

 2 Listen to the lecture about Planet X
and answer the questions.

   a. What is one reason
some scientists give that
Planet X exists?

   b. What are two theories about
what Planet X might be?

3 Listen again and decide if the
sentences are **T** (true) or **F** (false).

_____ **1.** Percival Lowell discovered that the planets Mercury and
Pluto did not follow the orbits they should have.

_____ **2.** Pluto is not big enough to create changes in the orbits
of Uranus and Neptune.

_____ **3.** If Planet X is located in the Oort cloud, then it will take
the planet five million years to orbit the sun once.

_____ **4.** Whitmire and Matese believe that Planet X is a cold, brown
dwarf star about two hundred million miles from the sun.

_____ **5.** The kind of telescope needed to prove the existence and
location of Planet X is already available.

Pronunciation

Intonation is related to stress and tone. It is also used to indicate a speaker's
assumption of what is new knowledge and what is shared knowledge. New
information often comes near the end of a sentence. A rising-falling
intonation pattern indicates new information in the statement.

> new information
>
> For homework, read about the <u>Oort cloud</u>.
>
> now-known, shared information   new information
>
> After you've read about the <u>Oort cloud</u>, compare it with the <u>Kuiper belt</u>.

4 Read the sentences and predict where the rising-falling pattern occurs by marking those words with arrows.

    a. Muller has suggested our sun has a distant companion star.

    b. He and his colleagues named this low-mass binary star Nemesis.

    c. They believe Nemesis affects the orbits of comets.

    d. These huge groups of comets are located in the Oort cloud.

    e. Moving through the Oort cloud, Nemesis sends the comets towards earth.

    f. Many scientists believe these comets have caused mass extinctions.

5 Listen to the sentences to check your predictions.

6 Work with a partner. Take turns reading the sentences aloud, focusing on the intonation at the end of the sentences.

Speak Out

STRATEGY **Citing Sources for Support** When participating in a discussion or meeting, it is important to support statements and opinions with facts. This can be accomplished by citing authoritative sources, such as experts in the field; articles from magazines, journals, and newspapers; reports; presentations; or other sources of information considered to be valid by the participants.

7 Read the dialogue and underline the factual support cited and the phrases that introduce the sources.

    BILL: So we're all in agreement, then?

    JOAN: Not quite, Bill. It's just that I think it's a risk too costly to take.

    BILL: Well, I'd like to point out that in the last division report, our design was described as "potentially valuable well beyond its cost."

    JOAN: Oh, really? When did the report come out?

    BILL: Last week.

    JACK: And Jake Martin, in his column in *Space Today*, said that robotic rovers are clearly providing data more cheaply than any other type of surface-focused vehicle at the current time.

    BILL: And, as you know, our design is considered ground-breaking. We've been nominated for the Robotics Design Award this year.

    JOAN: Well, OK. If all that doesn't give us credibility, what does?

8 All the statements below express support. However, not all of them cite sources. Check the statements below that do *not* provide factual support.

_____ **a.** I back you up on that 100 percent, Doug.

_____ **b.** Bradley's research confirmed Ford's 2001 results.

_____ **c.** A full 94 percent of the kids who went to NASA camp reported they loved it.

_____ **d.** Well, we're probably on the right track, don't you think?

_____ **e.** The report said the compound withstood 2,500° F.

_____ **f.** Nuñez was quoted on TV using that same estimate.

9 Work with a partner. Brainstorm supporting reasons and examples to support each side of the situation below. Then work in small groups with students acting as representatives for each side. As you present your statements and opinions, cite sources to support them.

SITUATION

Your school has received a large sum of money from a donor. The faculty would like to devote the money to developing a new science program. However, the parents want the same money to be used to construct a soccer field for the school.

READING and WRITING

Read About It

1 **Before You Read** Do you think that replicas of Earth's cities or farms will be established on distant planets in the future? Why or why not? Share your ideas with a partner.

STRATEGY ▶ **Applying Concepts to New Information** When reading for understanding, effective readers apply new information and compare it with what they already know. This helps the reader understand and utilize the new information.

2 Read the selection. As you read, underline the passages in which the author uses comparisons.

A Hotel with a Million Stars

Hotels in space, lunar settlements, space cruise liners . . . Sounds like science fiction, but this is actually the newly emerging industry of space tourism. Even hardened skeptics now admit that space tourism will probably become reality in the next fifty years. The American millionaire Dennis Tito made headlines by becoming the first space tourist, paying an estimated $20 million out of his own pocket for a ticket to the International Space Station Alpha.

(continued on next page)

(continued on next page)

Many surveys have in fact shown that as many as 80 percent of people younger than forty are interested in commercial space travel, and the majority would be willing to pay up to three months' salary for the experience. Ten percent would even pay a year's salary for the privilege of watching Earth from space.

The question is, however, whether the idea of commercial space travel is viable. One of the key issues is reducing the cost of fuel and, consequently, travel. Sending tourists into space is not far in terms of distance—it's just 100 miles away, straight up, which is less than half the distance between New York City and Washington, D.C. As it stands now, however, taking tourists on voyages into space would be in the price range of billions of dollars. Experts predict, however, that the cost of space travel will ultimately drop, just like that of video cassette recorders. When the first VCRs came out, people were paying close to $1,200 for them. Now you can buy them for less than $80.

Even though space travel will probably come about very slowly, a lot of the advance planning work is already in place. One of the most elaborate models has been proposed by a team from the University of Houston. The first stage in their proposal calls for a space factory which will be taking advantage of weightlessness and manufacturing products difficult or impossible to make on earth. The factory will be manned by robots, with periodic visits from space crews. Gradually, the factory will expand into a research laboratory which will provide a home for four to six technicians. The next stage will involve the development of a space media center, which will provide services for news organizations, film crews, and meteorologists. Eventually, the space media center will evolve into a "space spa," a place for space crews to stop and recuperate before flying off to other space locations. The final stage of the project foresees the expansion of the recuperation center into a space hotel for guests, with prospects of stunning views of Earth. This project seems realistic because by the time the space hotel comes into existence, the other phases of the project will have come into existence and paved the way for the orbiting hotel. In contrast, the Apollo lunar program from the 1960s was a fantastic achievement, but it left nothing but a flag on the moon and didn't further space travel in a direct way.

Once space tourism takes off, what can space travelers expect? Orbiting Earth in space, they will be staying in no ordinary

hotel. It would have a million stars—but no gravity. Even though there are ways to design the hotel so it would simulate the earth's gravity, weightlessness would be one of the main attractions, so why ruin the
55 fun, experts say? The hotels will be like ocean cruise liners, unhurriedly cruising through the vastness of space. Unlike cruise liners, though, the living accommodations might be closer to those of a base camp on Mount Everest than to those on a cruise ship like the Queen Elizabeth II. There will be no fancy dining or comfortable sleeping quarters. Visitors
60 will probably be sleeping in sleeping bags attached to the walls of tiny cabins. They'll be eating paper-plate dinners while their feet are secured to the floor to keep them from floating away from the table. They won't be taking any showers, but will be using wet wipes instead. The trips will probably last no more than two weeks. There will also
65 be outside excursions which will include guided space walks and day tours to orbiting research stations and the moon.

   Will space tourism actually become an industry? Most likely, yes. But probably only for closer destinations. Sending people to the moon would only take nine days, for example, but a voyage to Mars could
70 take almost three years. Only the future will tell how this dream of expanding space exploration will develop. One thing is certain, though. In the years to come, space will no longer be a final frontier for many of us.

3 The notes list some of the analogies the author makes, either implicitly or explicitly. Analyze the article and complete the notes.

Item		Is compared with
1. the distance from the earth to space	=	
2. the change in the cost of space travel	=	
3. the University of Houston project	=	
4. living accommodations in space	=	

4 Discuss these questions with a partner.
   a. What does market research indicate about interest in space tourism?
   b. What is currently the major obstacle to commercial space travel?
   c. In the model proposed by the University of Houston, what are the five phases in the development of a space hotel?

5 **Vocabulary Check** Match the words from the article with their meanings. Write the letters. Compare your responses with a partner's.

_____ **1.** hardened (line 3)

_____ **2.** viable (line 14)

_____ **3.** fuel (line 14)

_____ **4.** call for (line 27)

_____ **5.** foresee (line 38)

_____ **6.** stunning (line 40)

_____ **7.** pave the way (line 44)

a. understand (something) in advance

b. extremely beautiful

c. prepare for and make possible

d. cynical

e. strongly recommend

f. an energy source such as coal, gas, gasoline

g. make a fire

h. possible, practical

Think About It

6 If you could take a trip to any place in the Solar System, where would you choose to go? Why?

Write: Block Organization

STRATEGY Another way to structure information in essays of comparison and/or contrast is block-style organization. In block style, each item being compared or contrasted is treated in separate paragraphs. The first paragraph examines the first item being compared or contrasted, and the second paragraph examines the second item under discussion.

In an essay contrasting two views of the planet Mars, for example, the following block organization could apply in the support paragraphs.

Paragraph 1: Mars: 19th century beliefs	**Paragraph 2:** Mars: 20th century beliefs
a. intelligent life existed on the planet	**a.** no intelligent life exists on the planet
b. canals formed by living beings	**b.** canals formed naturally
c. giant sculpture of a face on the surface	**c.** giant face an optical illusion

7 **Write About It** Write a short paper contrasting the planets Mercury and Pluto. You can contrast any points you wish, such as size, temperature, distance from the sun, or orbit.

8 **Check Your Writing** Exchange your paper with a partner's. Use the questions below to give feedback to your partner. When you get your paper back, revise as necessary.

- Is there an introductory paragraph?
- Do the supporting paragraphs cover all of the first item before contrasting the second item with it?
- Is there a clear conclusion?

ADVENTURE VACATIONS

GETTING STARTED

Warm Up

What is your idea of a great vacation? Would you rather travel or relax at home? Many people are attracted to adventure vacations, which provide opportunities to experience strong emotions, thrills, and challenges.

1 How dangerous are these adventure vacations? Rank them in order of danger from **1** (most dangerous) to **8** (least dangerous). Share your ideas with a partner. Which ones appeal to you?

_____ a cave exploration trip   _____ mountain climbing

_____ a dinosaur dig   _____ a cowboy-style cattle drive

_____ a photographic safari   _____ a bicycling tour

_____ white-water rafting   _____ (your own idea)

2 Listen to Paula describe her vacation in the Philippines. Why did she go to the Philippines? What happened while she was there? Did she enjoy herself? Share your information with the class.

Figure It Out

3 Read the brochure about Anasazi Adventures.

The Vacation of a Lifetime!

Are you tired of hoping for the best but expecting the worst each year? When you write "Wish you were here." on all those postcards sent from boring beaches, do you wish *you weren't* there?

Now is the time to choose a vacation that will:

- 🐛 stimulate your senses
- 🐛 challenge your intellect
- 🐛 immerse you in an ancient culture
- 🐛 contribute to world knowledge

Anasazi Archaeological Adventures (A.A.A.)
Join an archaeological dig for artifacts from an ancient Anasazi site!

Surrounded by scenic beauty, you will experience the suspense of digging and the joy of uncovering authentic Anasazi artifacts dating from 700 to 1,500 years ago. You may find ancient arrowheads, axes, pots, jars, or ceremonial figurines. And the best part is that you will be recognized as the donor when you donate your findings to the community museum on site. Each dig is conducted by a professional archaeologist and carried out according to state and national guidelines concerning historic sites.

Contact: Mr. Bruno Loyola-Shantz (A.A.A.)
275 West Stone Street
Mystic Circle, Utah 84321
1-800-555-4962

4 **Vocabulary Check** Match the words on the left with their meanings on the right.

_____ **1.** stimulate   **a.** tension, excitement

_____ **2.** immerse   **b.** excavation, exploration

_____ **3.** artifacts   **c.** small, ornamental statue

_____ **4.** dig   **d.** awaken, engage

_____ **5.** suspense   **e.** patience, calm

_____ **6.** figurine   **f.** surround (one) with

g. objects made by human hands

Talk About It

 An airline passenger is discussing her vacation with a flight attendant. Work with a partner. Take turns being the flight attendant and the passenger. Ask and answer questions about vacation plans using the cues and the conversation as a model.

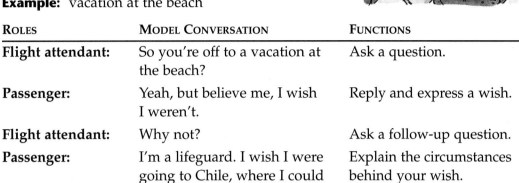

Example: vacation at the beach

ROLES	MODEL CONVERSATION	FUNCTIONS
Flight attendant:	So you're off to a vacation at the beach?	Ask a question.
Passenger:	Yeah, but believe me, I wish I weren't.	Reply and express a wish.
Flight attendant:	Why not?	Ask a follow-up question.
Passenger:	I'm a lifeguard. I wish I were going to Chile, where I could spend a week in the the snow!	Explain the circumstances behind your wish.

Vacation Plans

a. photo safari in the Amazon

b. bicycle tour of south of France

c. whitewater rafting trip

d. week of silent meditation

e. ballroom dance classes

f. (your own idea)

GRAMMAR

Omitting *If* in Conditional Sentences

When we talk about unreal or hypothetical situations, we can use the conditional. For emphasis we can omit the *if* and invert the subject and auxiliary verb.

First Conditional	**If Robert should invite** you on the safari, you'll need to buy a lot of equipment.	**Should Robert invite** you on a safari, you'll need to buy a lot of equipment.
Second Conditional	**If I were rich**, I would go on a world tour.	**Were I rich**, I would go on a world tour.
Third Conditional	**If Nicole had trained** more, she would have won.	**Had Nicole trained** more, she would have won.

1 Restate the sentences by inverting the subject and auxiliary verb instead of using *if*. Compare your answers with a partner's.

Example: Because he didn't recover from his injuries, he wasn't able to participate in the climbing expedition.

  Had he recovered, he would have been able to participate
  in the expedition.

a. Ellen didn't book her flight in advance for the trip to Egypt, so she had to pay a lot of money for a last-minute ticket.

_____

b. You probably won't ever go on a boat tour of the Amazon. But if you do, don't forget your mosquito repellent.

_____

c. The avalanche wasn't big. Otherwise, the whole expedition would have been swept away.

_____

d. I'm glad the wind wasn't stronger. Otherwise, it might have overturned the raft.

_____

e. In the unlikely event you see an elephant, take pictures.

_____

f. I didn't know how to ski, so I couldn't take the same slopes as you.

_____

Wish

We use *wish* to express desire or regret about a hypothetical or imaginary situation. We are fairly sure the situation will not easily change. The main clause is followed by a *wish clause*, similar in form to the second and third conditionals.

For wishes about the present, the verb of the wish clause is in the simple past or in the past progressive.

Wishes About the Present		
	Main Clause	**Wish Clause**
I don't know how to surf.	I wish	I **knew** how to surf.
Liz is afraid of heights.	Liz wishes	she **weren't** so afraid of heights.
I am not sailing.	I wish	I **were sailing** now.

For wishes about the past, the verb of the wish clause is in the past perfect or past perfect progressive. Wishes about past possibilities use *could have* + past participle.

Wishes About the Past		
	Main Clause	**Wish Clause**
Chris didn't visit the Taj Mahal when he was in India.	Chris wishes	he **had visited** the Taj Mahal when he was in India.
As a child I always got seasick on boats.	I wish	I **hadn't gotten** seasick on boats as a child.
Mary wasn't able to travel to China when she was young.	Mary wishes	she **could have traveled** to China when she was young.

To wish for something to be different in the future, we use *would* in the wish clause.

Wishes About the Future		
	Main Clause	**Wish Clause**
Sometimes governments stop explorers from entering a country.	I wish	governments **wouldn't stop** explorers from entering a country.

 On a separate piece of paper, write a few wishes about the following topics. Then share your wishes with a partner.

- Something you would like to change about a person you know.
- Something you would like to change about your childhood.

If Only

If only has the same meaning as *I wish,* but is more emphatic. The clause with *if only* often stands alone.

The Present	If only I **knew** how to swim!	I wish I **knew** how to swim. (But I don't.)
Present Ability	If only I **could ride** a horse!	I wish I **could ride** a horse. (But I can't)
The Past	If only I **had accepted** the scholarship to study in Canada last year.	I wish I **had accepted** the scholarship to study in Canada last year. (But I hadn't.)
Past Ability	If only I **could have rented** a car when I was in Spain!	I wish I **could have rented** a car when I was in Spain! (But I wasn't able to.)
The Future	If only it **would stop** snowing so hard, we could go snowboarding.	I wish it **would stop** snowing so hard so we could go snowboarding. (But it won't.)

3 The members of a poorly organized mountain-climbing expedition are complaining about things that went wrong or are going wrong. Rewrite their complaints using *if only*. Compare your answers with a partner's.

   a. "We didn't take enough oxygen with us. We had to borrow some from other climbers."

   b. "Last night I couldn't sleep at all because of the cold."

   c. "The assistant guide is so rude! I'm afraid to speak to him."

   d. "I'm completely exhausted. How am I going to continue?"

   e. "I can't feel my legs. They are completely numb from the cold."

   f. "The cell phone doesn't work. How are we going to ask for help?"

   g. "The guides didn't bring a spare compass. What if this one gets lost?"

 4 **Check Your Understanding** Use the pictures below to complete the sentences. Share your ideas with a partner.

   a. "Had I known _____"

      "I wish _____"

      "If only_____"

   b. "If only _____"

      "Should I _____"

      "I wish _____"

   c. "I wish _____"

      "Should _____"

      "If only_____"

 5 **Express Yourself** Often in life we regret things that we haven't done or things we have. Think of three situations in which you wish you had acted differently. In small groups, talk about these regrets using *I wish . . ., If only . . ., Had I known . . .*

LISTENING and SPEAKING

Listen: Newsworthy

1 **Before You Listen** If you could build your vacation around a major world event, such as a film festival or the Olympics, what would it be? Who would you take with you?

STRATEGY **Identifying Tone** When listening for critical analysis or personal interpretation, effective listeners focus on the speaker's tone to understand his or her attitude toward the topics under discussion. A speaker's tone can signal agreement, neutrality, or complete disagreement with the actual message delivered.

2 Listen to three commentaries by different radio announcers. What kind of event is each announcer describing? Write the number on the line in the correct picture. There is one extra picture.

3 Listen again. Which word best describes the tone of each commentary? Write the number of the commentary on the line.

_____ **a.** serious

_____ **b.** enthusiastic

_____ **c.** disappointed

Pronunciation

Thought Groups When we speak, we pause not only after sentences but also within sentences. These pauses occur after we say a series of words, phrases, or clauses that belong together logically and grammatically. These groups of words are called *thought groups*. Thought groups are marked not only by pauses, but also by intonation.

> **A:** When you go scuba diving | you need a wet suit, | goggles, | and a snorkel. |
> **B:** What about air tanks?
> **A:** Oh, yeah, | that's the most important thing!|

4 Predict the thought groups by marking them with a line on either side of the thought group. Compare your answers with a partner's.

A: Have you heard about *Kon-Tiki*?

B: No, what is that?

A: It's the name of a famous raft built by Norwegian scientist Thor Heyerdahl in the 1940s.

B: Why is it so famous?

A: Because Heyerdahl and his crew sailed from Peru to Polynesia on that raft.

B: Wow, that's about 5,000 miles! Why did they do it?

A: The crew wanted to demonstrate that people could have sailed from South America to Polynesia hundreds of years ago.

B: Well, he sure made his point! By the way, who or what is *Kon-Tiki*?

A: *Kon-Tiki* is an ancient sun god.

5 Listen to the conversation to check your answers.

6 Practice the conversation with a partner, focusing on thought groups.

Speak Out

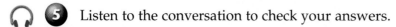 **Providing Support** Many ideas and suggestions arise during the course of a meeting or discussion. After analysis of these ideas, participants show their support for the idea, solution, or concept they think will best serve the group.

7 Underline the sentences that show support in the conversation below.

TED: And that's why I feel our best choice is to restructure the whole project.

SUE: But that will take so much time! Time we don't have!

BILL: Well, why don't we consider eliminating stage four of the project and leave the rest the way it is now?

SUE: You mean do away with it completely?

BILL: Yes, at least for now. It would simplify our procedures and save us time too.

TED: I feel strongly that stage four should stay, but in a modified form.

SUE: Well, I find Bill's suggestion to be the best in terms of efficiency.

PAT: I'm for Bill's solution too. It will even help in terms of cost.

8 Check the expressions that show support for an idea or solution.

_____ **a.** I'm throwing my weight behind Carlos.

_____ **b.** I'd appreciate your looking into that for next time.

_____ **c.** I think you have a valid point there.

_____ **d.** How do you interpret it, John?

_____ **e.** You've got my vote, Jaehak.

_____ **f.** I'd like to suggest an additional meeting on this.

_____ **g.** Frank's idea should be given our full consideration.

_____ **h.** Debbie is right on target—let's go with her solution.

_____ **i.** I have to back Howard on this one.

_____ **j.** I'll get back to you on that tomorrow.

9 Work with a partner. Brainstorm supporting reasons and examples to support each side of the discussion below. Then work in small groups with representatives of each side. Take turns showing support for the ideas and suggestions you like.

> **SITUATION**
>
> A committee is meeting to decide about the class trip. Some want to plan a traditional outing with visits to museums, concerts, and other cultural events. Others want to design a completely different kind of class trip involving adventure or risk.

READING and WRITING

Read About It

1 **Before You Read** Why do you think people risk their lives climbing mountains, cutting their way through jungles, or exploring the depths of a cave? What qualities should a successful explorer have? Share your ideas with a partner.

STRATEGY **Recognizing Comparisons and Contrasts** When reading for critical analysis and personal interpretation, efficient readers focus on similarities and differences between objects, people, or ideas that writers have pointed out. Recognizing comparisons and contrasts enables the reader to relate something new to something familiar and form a mental picture of the subject.

2 Read the article. As you read, note how the author makes comparisons and contrasts.

Junko Tabei: Conquerer of Mountains
by Jerdine Nolen-Harold

Imagine that you are the leader of a mountain-climbing expedition that will take you to the top of the world—the peak of Mount Everest, 8,850 meters (29,035 feet) high. Thin air, freezing winds, and numbingly cold temperatures stand between you and your goal. You're in your tent in the frigid cold when
5 an avalanche strikes. You are buried under a block of ice. You cannot move. You can barely breathe. What would you wish for in those last moments?

(continued on next page)

For Junko Tabei, the first woman to climb Mount Everest, her wish was another chance to see the family she had left behind in Japan. Her thoughts went to her three-year-old daughter. She hoped her little girl would somehow learn to get along without her mother. Tabei then lost consciousness for about six minutes, while her Sherpa guide dug her out.

With no intention of giving up, she continued climbing, despite the injuries she had received in the avalanche. It would take all of the tenacity, strength, and will she could summon to become the first woman to conquer Mount Everest. She remembers the feeling when she reached the summit. When asked if reaching the top was everything she had expected, she said, "There was no enjoyment, just relief. I was very, very happy that I didn't have to climb anymore."

Mount Everest is said to be unforgiving. Temperatures can plunge to well below freezing. The mountain's extremely steep faces, together with its strong winds, thin air, and deep crevasses, make the climb incredibly dangerous. Climbers must be experienced mountaineers in top physical condition. As they reach higher altitudes, they have to stop to let their bodies adjust to the lack of oxygen. In addition, the climbers have to carry heavy equipment with them in their ascent. These hardships have contributed to the challenges all Everest climbers face. Over sixty-nine people have died while trying to achieve their goal. Eleven expeditions had tried and failed to reach the top before Sir Edmund Hillary and Tenzing Norgay, a local Sherpa, did so on May 10, 1953.

Climbing Mount Everest takes two days or more, but months or even years of preparation are required before the climb begins. Money for supplies, transportation to Nepal, Sherpa guides, and climbing fees charged by the Nepalese government must be found. For Tabei, the preparations were almost as daunting as the climb. While seeking funding for her expedition, Tabei approached a large corporation, which told her that it was impossible for a woman to climb Mount Everest and that she ought to go home and take care of her baby! If only they had realized that their response would make her more determined to succeed than ever! She began to teach piano from her home and later received sponsorship from a television network to pay for her trip.

Tabei's expedition included fifteen Japanese women and over fifteen tons of supplies and equipment, including tents, sleeping bags, food, stoves, fuel, clothing, climbing tools, and oxygen. Like climbers before them, they established a series of base camps up the side of the mountain. Climbers worked in groups moving equipment up the mountain from one camp to the next, returning at night to the lower camp for a day of rest at a warmer altitude.

Tabei was thirty-five years old when she climbed Mount Everest. Since then, the diminutive woman (under five feet tall) has become the first female to

50 tower over the highest mountains on six of the world's seven continents, including Mt. Blanc in Europe, Mt. Kilimanjaro in Africa, Mt. Aconcagua in South America, Mt. McKinley in North America, and Vinson Massif in Antarctica. Hoping to reach her personal goal of covering all seven continents, she is awaiting permission from the Indonesian government to climb Mt. Jaya. After
55 that, her goal is to climb the highest mountain in each country in the world. She expects to reach that ambitious goal around the year 2020.

   Tabei became interested in mountaineering at an early age. When she was ten years old, she climbed a small mountain while on a class field trip. That experience touched her profoundly and motivated her to continue seeking ways
60 to accomplish her dream of climbing the world's great peaks. She has received awards and congratulations from the prime minister of Japan, the king of Nepal, and other heads of state. She gives interviews, lectures at universities, and has appeared on many television talk shows. She is no longer dependent on corporate sponsors, because the income from her lectures and appearances
65 covers expenses for her cherished expeditions. Tabei has served as a role model for her children and other adventurous women as well, and she is quick to encourage all those with a love of the world's heights to pursue their dreams as she did hers.

 The chart contains some items the author compares, implicitly (implied) or explicitly (clearly stated), in the article. Analyze the comparisons and complete the chart. Label each comparison **I** (implicit) or **E** (explicit).

The author compares	with	Comparison Type
1. the difficulty of the climb		
2. Tabei's short height		
3. raising money by teaching piano lessons		

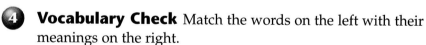 **Vocabulary Check** Match the words on the left with their meanings on the right.

_____ **1.** expedition (line 1)   **a.** fall abruptly, become lower

_____ **2.** barely (line 6)   **b.** not anymore, not now

_____ **3.** tenacity (line 16)   **c.** money for expenses

_____ **4.** summon (line 17)   **d.** just a little, scarcely

_____ **5.** plunge (line 22)   **e.** loved, valued

_____ **6.** crevasses (line 24)   **f.** determination to succeed

_____ **7.** daunting (line 36)   **g.** small in size or stature

_____ **8.** funding (line 36)   **h.** call up, gather together

_____ **9.** diminutive (line 49)   **i.** narrow cracks, openings

_____ **10.** cherished (line 65)   **j.** exploratory trip, travel

                  k. challenging

Think About It

 Would you leave young children at home so you could look for adventure? Is Junko's behavior brave or foolish? Why? Compare your ideas with your partner's.

Write: Essay of Contrast

An essay of comparison or contrast may be organized block style. All information about one of the items being compared or contrasted is presented first, in one paragraph or section, and then all the information about the second item is presented in a separate paragraph or section. If the essay is simply descriptive, the writer then brings the essay to a close. If the essay is persuasive, the writer then argues for a preference for one of the items being compared or contrasted.

 Work with a partner. Brainstorm items you would include in a block-style paper analyzing the differences between educational vacations and adventure vacations. Make an outline for the essay and then compare your ideas with those of another pair.

 When composing an essay of contrast, effective writers use transition words and expressions to show how the items under discussion are different.

in contrast	unlike
on the contrary	whereas
on the one hand . . . on the other hand	while

Examples:

1. **Unlike** large ocean cruise boats which have to remain a safe distance from the shore, the smaller cruise boats can get close to the glaciers so that you get a close-up view.
2. People on regular tours to the pyramids only get to see the results of the archaeologists' finds. **In contrast**, people on archaeological digs actually get to participate in these finds.

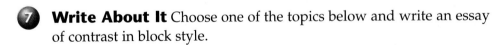

 Write About It Choose one of the topics below and write an essay of contrast in block style.

traditional vs. cycling vacations	vacations taken alone vs. on a tour
vacations at the beach vs. the mountains	worst vs. best vacation experience
vacations at home vs. abroad	(your own idea)

 Check Your Writing Exchange your paper with a partner. Use the guidelines on block-style organization you have studied to give feedback to your partner. When you receive your own paper, revise as necessary.

GETTING STARTED

Warm Up

As a learner of English, you are personally experiencing both the joys and frustrations of communicating in a new language. At some time in your study, you have probably used translation as a way to clarify meaning.

1 How have you used translation? In what circumstances? What have been some advantages and disadvantages of translation?

2 How often do you translate English into your native language? Have you ever had a misunderstanding caused by a poor translation? What were the circumstances? What happened as a result?

3 Listen to an interview from the radio show *Book Talk*. What is the title of the new book? What is the main idea of the book?

Figure It Out

 José, Lisa, and Fred are discussing a TV program on mistranslations. Read their conversation.

LISA: Hey, did you see that program on translation mistakes last night?

JOSÉ: No, I was watching a football game.

FRED: I saw it. It was hilarious.

5   **JOSÉ:** What was so funny?

LISA: Well, they talked about pitfalls people face when they use their dictionaries to do literal translations.

JOSÉ: Like when John F. Kennedy went to Berlin and said he was "ein Berliner," which in German is a pastry instead of a citizen of Berlin?

10 **FRED:** Well, sort of. These were mainly advertising bloopers that American companies had made when they tried to market their products in other languages.

JOSÉ: Oh, that sounds like fun. What were some?

FRED: Well, of course there's the case of when the pope visited Miami,
15   and one company made souvenir T-shirts in Spanish that, instead of saying people had seen the pope (el Papa), they said that people had seen the potato (la papa).

LISA: And what about the cola maker that mistranslated its slogan into Chinese so it said that using their product would bring people's
20   ancestors back from the grave?

FRED: My favorite was the baby food one.

LISA: Oh yeah, that was a really good one!

JOSÉ: What was that?

FRED: Well, it wasn't technically a mistranslation, but it was a big cultural
25   blooper. You know that baby food company that has a picture of a really cute baby on its labels? Well, they used the same label when they tried to sell their baby food in Africa a few years ago. Now their thinking was that even though most people there didn't read, they would use the picture on the label to figure out what the product was
30   for. But they didn't realize that the custom in the country is to put pictures on the label of what is actually *inside* the jar. So, instead of customers thinking the jars contained food for babies, they thought the jars contained food...

JOSÉ: ... made of babies. I guess they didn't sell too much of that! I love
35   these stories.

5 **Vocabulary Check** Match the words on the right with their correct meanings on the left.

_____ **1.** hilarious (line 4)   **a.** product name tag

_____ **2.** pitfalls (line 6)   **b.** mistake

_____ **3.** pastry (line 9)   **d.** danger, problems

_____ **4.** blooper (line 10)   **c.** kind, sort

_____ **5.** ancestors (line 20)   **e.** a small, sweet cake

_____ **6.** grave (line 20)   **f.** dead relatives

_____ **7.** label (line 26)   **g.** extremely funny

                                          h. burial place

Talk About It

 6 A professor and a student are discussing the meanings of memorable quotes from important people. Work with a partner. Take turns being the professor and the student, and discuss the quotations from the people below. Use the conversation as a model.

Example: Gandhi: "You cannot shake hands with a clenched fist."

ROLES	MODEL CONVERSATION	FUNCTIONS
Professor:	Gandhi said that you couldn't shake hands with a clenched fist.	Report what someone said.
Student:	What do you think he meant by that?	Ask for an interpretation.
Professor:	I think he meant that violence couldn't solve problems.	Give an explanation.

<u>Quotations</u>

a. La Rochefoucauld: "All of us have strength enough to bear the misfortunes of others."

b. Confucius: "Take a job you love, and you will never have to work a day in your life."

c. Cervantes: "A closed mouth catches no flies."

d. Socrates: "An unexamined life is not worth living."

e. Molière: "Envious men may die, but envy never does."

f. (your own idea)

Reported Statements

We use reported speech to describe someone else's words or thoughts. In reported speech, we change the speaker's words by changing first-person pronouns and by changing adverbs of time and place. If the reporting verb (*say, tell, report*) is in the present tense, the tense in the following clause stays the same. If it is in the past, the verb in the following clause is shifted.

Direct Statements	Reported Statements
"I **am translating** a book about the Mayan civilization."	My colleague **says** (that) she **is translating** a book about the Mayan civilization.
"Gregory Rabassa **translated** *The War of the Saints* **last year**."	The publisher **told** me (that) Gregory Rabassa **had translated** *The War of the Saints* **the previous year**.
"This translation **will be** time-consuming."	He **said** (to me)(that) the translation **would be** time-consuming.
"You **can talk** to the translator in his office next week."	She **told** me (that) I **could talk** to the translator in his office the following week.

1 These signs are all examples of comic mistranslations into English. Work with a partner. Report what the signs say and what you think they *meant* to say.

Example: The Hong Kong dentist sign says that teeth are extracted by the latest Methodists. It meant to say that teeth were extracted by the latest methods.

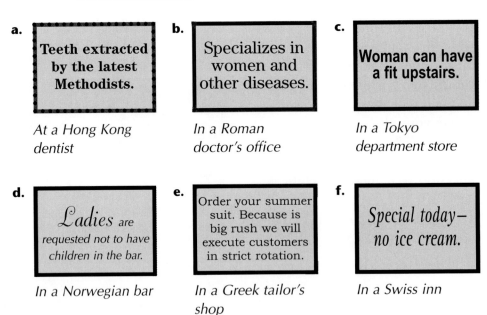

a.
Teeth extracted by the latest Methodists.

At a Hong Kong dentist

b.
Specializes in women and other diseases.

In a Roman doctor's office

c.
Woman can have a fit upstairs.

In a Tokyo department store

d.
Ladies are requested not to have children in the bar.

In a Norwegian bar

e.
Order your summer suit. Because is big rush we will execute customers in strict rotation.

In a Greek tailor's shop

f.
Special today— no ice cream.

In a Swiss inn

Reporting Verbs

Say and tell are reporting words with neutral connotations. When statements are reported with *say*, they follow the pattern: *say* (to someone) (*that*) + clause. *Tell* follows the pattern: *tell* someone (*that*) + clause. Other reporting verbs follow the *say* or *tell* pattern.

Reporting Verbs Similar in Use to *Say* (to someone) (that)			
admit	complain	mention	report
announce	confess	point out	shout
brag	explain	remark	state
comment	indicate	reply	whisper

Reporting Verbs Similar in Use to *Tell* (someone that)			
assure	inform	persuade	reassure
convince	notify	remind	

2 The paragraph below is from an instructor's talk at a workshop on translation. Rewrite each sentence as reported speech using a variety of appropriate reporting verbs.

Example:

He informed the class that the previous year he had worked on translating Chinese poetry.

I worked on translating Chinese poetry into English last year.
I was also translating a book about the Ming Dynasty, which is
due to appear in this country next year. This is not the first work
I've translated from Chinese. My translation of *The Chinese Diaries*
sold here and in Asia last year. It didn't have as many sales as we
expected because it didn't get enough publicity. Of course, having
knowledge about the culture behind the language is just as
important as knowing the words of the language. For example, the
Chinese title of the film *The English Patient* was *Don't Ask Me Who
I Am* because Chinese audiences weren't familiar with the book and
would not have gone to see a movie with the translated title of
The Sick Englishman.

Reporting Questions

To report an information question, we use question word + clause.
To report a yes/no question, we use *if* or *whether* + clause. When we report questions, we use statement word order.

Direct Questions	Reported Questions
a. "**When can you** finish the project?"	He wondered **when I could** finish the project.
b. **When did you** live in Barcelona?	He asked **when I had lived** in Barcelona.
c. "**Who recommended** her for this job?"	He wondered **who had recommended** her for that job.
d. "**Will you be able to** complete the translation on time?	He wanted to know **whether I would be able to** complete the translation on time.
e. "**Have you had** any experience translating from Hungarian?	He wanted to know **if I had** had any experience translating from Hungarian.

3 Work with a partner. On a separate sheet of paper, rewrite this conversation in reported speech.

A: What is the difference between a translator and an interpreter?

B: Translators generally work on a written text. Interpreters translate what a speaker is saying simultaneously, usually at a conference or business meeting.

A: What is the typical rate for translation per 1,000 words?

B: It's hard to say because it depends on the languages involved, the subject matter, the complexity and length of the text, as well as the time available for translation.

A: How long will it take to get about fifty pages translated?

B: It depends on the subject matter and complexity of the text. But, in general, a translator can produce about ten to twelve pages a day.

A: What is a "source text" and what is a "target text?"

B: "Source text" refers to the text in the original language requiring translation. "Target text" is the text after it has been translated into the second language.

A: Are there automated translation systems that work?

B: Well, yes, more and more translation software is appearing on the market. But I don't think it will ever take the place of an actual translator because there is just too much translation that depends on human judgment.

4 **Check Your Understanding** Work with a partner. Choose one joke each and report it to your partner using reported speech.

JOKE 1

Two translators on a ship were talking.

"Can you swim?" asked one.

"No," said the other, "but I can shout for help in nine languages."

JOKE 2

Two software developers were talking.

"The phrase *out of sight, out of mind* was translated by automatic translation software from English into Japanese and back into English again," said one of them.

"And what was the final product?" asked the other.

"*The invisible idiot.*"

 5 **Express Yourself** Decide if you **A** (agree) or **D** (disagree) with the statements below. Then, work in small groups and have a brief discussion on the statements. When you finish, report your discussion to another group.

_____ **a.** Translators should stay as close to the original texts' words as possible.

_____ **b.** With the advancements made in automated translation systems, human translators, publishers, and language instructors could lose their jobs in the future.

_____ **c.** Poetry shouldn't be translated because a person can feel its full beauty only in the original.

_____ **d.** Translators should get more credit for what they do because their job is almost as important as that of the authors.

LISTENING and SPEAKING

Listen: One World, One Language?

1 **Before You Listen** Some people think that most of humanity's problems would disappear if we all spoke one language, constructed especially for that purpose. Do you believe a global language would help the world communicate better? Why or why not?

STRATEGY **Drawing Conclusions** When listening for critical analysis or creative action, effective listeners focus on key ideas to draw conclusions from the information. Conclusions can be drawn from information that is directly stated or only implied.

2 Listen to a panel of professors discussing the language Esperanto. Note the key ideas and interesting details. Then use your notes to mark the statements below **T** (true) or **F** (false). Compare your answers with a partner's.

_____ **a.** Esperanto is an artificial language.

_____ **b.** Experts agree on how many Esperanto speakers there are in the world today.

_____ **c.** Esperanto is intended to be used as a first language.

_____ **d.** Throughout history, the language of the dominant political and economic power has always been the global language.

3 Listen again and answer the questions. Then discuss your answers in small groups.

a. According to the panelists, why is Esperanto easier to learn than English?

b. In the panelists' opinions, what other features of Esperanto make it superior to English ?

c. The panelists claim that a Korean and an English speaker would have to use the same amount of effort to learn Esperanto. Do you agree? Why or why not?

4 Based on the information you have heard and the conclusions you have drawn about Esperanto, which of the following actions would you consider? Check the boxes. Discuss your answers with a partner.

☐ I am going to read more about Esperanto.

☐ I am willing to argue in favor of world use of Esperanto.

☐ I am going to try to take a class in Esperanto.

☐ I am going to give up studying English to study Esperanto.

☐ I will neither promote nor discourage use of Esperanto.

Pronunciation

5 Predict which words will receive emotive stress by placing an arrow above them.

A: The other day I met Sandra Cisneros, the famous Mexican-American writer.

B: No kidding! She's very famous, right?

A: Yeah. She asked me to translate her latest stories into Portuguese.

B: No way! She asked you to translate for her? What did you say?

A: I said no. I said yes, of course.

6 Listen to the dialogue to check your predictions.

7 Work with a partner. Take turns reading the dialogue, focusing on pitch and emotion.

Speak Out

STRATEGY **Closing a Discussion** An effective discussion manager helps shape the progress of a meeting so that key issues have been discussed by the end of the meeting. The leader reminds participants of the time (time management). At the end, the leader briefly summarizes what decisions were made (summarizing the discussion), mentions points to be continued in the next meeting (previewing the next meeting's agenda), and thanks the group for their participation.

Closing Tactics	
Zack, time is running short, so please be as brief as possible.	(the meeting will end soon, and there are more items to discuss)
Summing up, we have decided to offer a class analyzing artificial languages for next year.	(the participants are reminded of the group's decision)
So, folks, two weeks from now, we'll meet with our research on which languages to include in the syllabus for the new course.	(the participants are reminded of the content of the next discussion)

8 Decide if these expressions are used for **T** (time management),
S (summarizing the discussion), or **P** (previewing the next meeting's agenda).

_____ **1.** I'd appreciate your keeping it short, William.

_____ **2.** Phase 3 of our plan will be discussed next time.

_____ **3.** In conclusion, we have eliminated parts two, three, and five and decided to keep the rest.

_____ **4.** It's almost 3:00 P.M., so everyone has one minute to repeat his or her opinion before voting.

_____ **5.** I'd appreciate it if all of you could limit yourselves to five minutes or so.

_____ **6.** To recap, the group will postpone a decision on section 2 of the contract until we get clarification from above.

_____ **7.** We'll look at preliminary results of the survey on the 18th.

_____ **8.** So, to wrap up, we have allocated funds for proposals B, F, and H. Good work.

9 Work in small groups. Discuss any topic in this unit. Take turns closing the discussion by attending to time, summarizing the discussion, or previewing the next meeting.

READING and WRITING

Read About It

1 **Before You Read** You are going to read two versions of a poem about a caged panther. Describe a zoo that you especially liked or disliked. How do animals react when they are kept in small spaces?

The ideal translation resembles a window through which we can behold the original text. The better the translator has done his job, the less aware we are of his work.

STRATEGY ▶ **Focusing on Language Choice and Style** When reading translated literature for critical analysis and appreciation, it is important to focus on language choice and style. Translators must decide if they want to use a literal translation or a liberal translation. In a literal translation, each word is translated separately. In a liberal translation, the general meaning of a phrase or sentence is translated.

2 Read two translations of the poem "The Panther" by Rainer Maria Rilke on the next page. As you read, compare the differences.

The Panther
Jardin des Plantes, Paris

VERSION 1

His sight from ever gazing through the bars
has grown so blunt that it sees nothing more.
It seems to him that thousands of bars are
before him, and behind them nothing merely.

5 The easy motion of his supple stride,
which turns about the smallest circle,
is like a dance of strength about a center
in which a mighty will stands stupefied.

Only sometimes when the pupil's film
10 soundlessly opens . . . then one image fills
and glides through the quiet tension of the
limbs into the heart and ceases and is still.

© 1940 BY C.F. MACINTYRE

VERSION 2

His vision, from the constantly passing bars,
has grown so weary that it cannot hold
anything else. It seems to him there are
a thousand bars; and behind the bars, no world.

5 As he paces in cramped circles, over and over,
the movement of his powerful soft strides
is like a ritual dance around a center
in which a mighty will stands paralyzed.

Only at times, the curtain of the pupils
10 lifts, quietly—An image enters in,
rushes down through the tensed, arrested
muscles, plunges into the heart and is gone.

© 1982 BY STEPHEN MITCHELL

VERSION 1

 Vocabulary Check Match
the words on the left with their
meanings on the right.

____ **1.** gazing (line 1)   **a.** arms and
____ **2.** blunt (line 2)   legs
____ **3.** supple (line 5)   **b.** graceful
____ **4.** stride (line 5)   **c.** eyelid
____ **5.** will (line 8)   **d.** spirit
____ **6.** stupefied (line 8) **e.** step
____ **7.** pupil's film   **f.** dull
       (line 9)   **g.** stop
____ **8.** limbs (line 12)   **h.** looking
____ **9.** cease (line 12)   **i.** confused
                          j. only,
                              nothing
                              more than

VERSION 2

____ **1.** weary (line 2)   **a.** small,
____ **2.** pace (line 5)   confined
____ **3.** cramped (line 5) **b.** extremely
____ **4.** paralyzed (line 8)   tired
____ **5.** arrested (line 11) **c.** stopped
____ **6.** plunge (line 12)   **d.** walk back
                              and forth
                           e. drop down
                              sharply
                           f. unable to
                              move
                           g. stiff

Underline the different words each translator used to name the same concept (for example, *sight* and *vision*). Work with a partner. Compare your answers and discuss these questions.

a. Why did they choose different words?

b. Are the sentences the same length in each poem?

c. Which version do you like better? Why?

d. What is the main idea of Rilke's poem?

Think About It

 Many people aren't sure how poetry can relate to their own lives or how they should approach it. Are you comfortable reading it? Would you consider writing it? Why or why not?

Write: Self- and Peer Editing

Editing is an important part of writing. Self-editing and peer editing require careful planning to be effective.

 Before finalizing your paper, it is important to edit it. Focus on content, organization, and style, and then proofread it for grammar and mechanics (capitalization, punctuation).

Content

Is the topic worth reading/writing about? Are the ideas presented logically? Are they relevant? Are the purpose and audience clear?

Organization

Does the essay have a title? Is there an introductory paragraph with a clear thesis statement? Does everything in the essay relate to the main idea? Do the body paragraphs support the thesis with facts, examples, and authoritative opinions? Is there a concluding paragraph?

Style

Is the style appropriate and consistent? Are there varieties of sentence types? Is the vocabulary appropriate?

Grammar

Do the subjects and their verbs agree? Are verb tenses used accurately? Is the word order correct?

Mechanics

Are the spelling and punctuation correct?

 Write About It Write a short essay comparing and contrasting one of the following:

- the two versions of the Rilke poem on page 157
- animal life in the zoo and in the wild

  Check Your Writing Work with a partner. Exchange your papers. Use the list of questions above to edit each other's work and offer constructive criticism. When you have received feedback, revise as necessary.

GRAMMAR

STRATEGY   **IDENTIFYING DISTRACTORS** Many standardized tests require test takers to select the correct answer from a choice of three or four. If you can identify the incorrect answers first, it is easier to determine the correct one. Look carefully at the context and decide which answers you can eliminate immediately.

A Circle the letter of the best answer to complete each sentence.

1. Interviewer: I have with me today Elisio Cortez from the Continental Space Agency to discuss ethics and space exploration. Most space exploration scientists recognize that people _____ ethics for as long as space exploration exists. What do you think, Elisio?   A B Ⓒ D
   - **(A)** will talk to
   - **(B)** will have talked
   - **(C)** will be discussing
   - **(D)** will have discussed

2. Elisio: I agree. _____ a debate on this issue in every decision made about space exploration, we would one day regret it.   A B C D
   - **(A)** If we had included
   - **(B)** Had we included
   - **(C)** Were we not to include
   - **(D)** If we would not to include

3. Interviewer: You told me that next week you _____ an ethics workshop.   A B C D
   - **(A)** attend
   - **(B)** will attending
   - **(C)** were attending
   - **(D)** would be attending

4. Elisio: Yes. By next weekend, I believe _____ most of the benefits and costs of space exploration and colonization.   A B C D
   - **(A)** we will explore
   - **(B)** we will be exploring
   - **(C)** we will have explored
   - **(D)** we would be exploring

5. Interviewer: _____ you could find a way to eliminate those costs.   A B C D
   - **(A)** Had
   - **(B)** If only
   - **(C)** If there were
   - **(D)** If there would be

6. Elisio: We all _____ possible, but none of us truly believes that we can do more than reduce the costs as much as possible.   A B C D
   - **(A)** are wishing that is
   - **(B)** wish that to be
   - **(C)** wish that were
   - **(D)** wished that was

7. Elisio: We do hope, however, that _____ to this issue, we will be able to better predict preferred future courses of action.   A B C D
   - **(A)** should be allocated enough funds
   - **(B)** should enough funds be allocated
   - **(C)** had enough funds been allocated
   - **(D)** if enough funds would be allocated

8. Elisio: ____ more focused on future problems when space exploration   A B C D
    first began, we would have been able to avoid some of the mistakes
    we've already made.
    (A) If we are   **(C)** We had been
    (B) Had we been   **(D)** Would we have been

STRATEGY ▶ **LOOK FOR TIME EXPRESSIONS** Often in grammar tests, a time expression clearly indicates the
order of events and the correct verb tenses. Look for time expressions and use them to
decide which action came first, which came second, and which came last. By ordering the
events in your mind, you'll be able to identify any mistakes in verb tense more easily.

B Each sentence has four underlined words or phrases. One of these underlined words
   or phrases is incorrect. Circle the letter of the word or phrase that is incorrect

1. Last week my friend <u>told</u> me that she <u>will have signed up</u>   A Ⓑ C D
               A   B

    wilderness adventure course because she <u>had always wondered</u> how she
                                                      C

    <u>would deal</u> with extreme physical challenges.
       D

2. When I <u>asked</u> her which organization she <u>has signed up</u> with, she <u>told</u>   A B C D
             A   B   C

    me its name <u>was</u> Outward Bound.
                  D

3. I told her that I <u>had been interested</u> in Outward Bound for a while myself,   A B C D
                           A

    and that <u>I had known</u> <u>she was joining</u>, <u>I would have signed up</u> with her.
                  B   C   D

4. She <u>replied me</u> that there <u>was</u> still space on her trip and,   A B C D
            A   B

    <u>convinced me</u> to look into going along, so I called Outward Bound
         C

    and asked if I could <u>speak</u> to someone there that afternoon.
                            D

5. As I approached their office, I <u>thought</u>, "<u>By the time</u> this interview is   A B C D
                                        A   B

    finished, <u>I'll be knowing</u> if this is something I <u>will be able to go</u> or not."
                    C   D

6. The first thing I noticed was a poster with one person saying to another,   A B C D

   "I'm tired of beach and skiing vacations. <u>If only</u> I <u>can go</u> on an adventure
                                       A   **B**

   where I <u>could test</u> my limits and <u>learn</u> new skills."
             C   **D**

7. The Outward Bound person I <u>met</u> with <u>asked me</u> <u>if I have</u> ever   A B C D
                               A   **B**   **C**

   <u>wondered that</u> myself.
       D

8. He <u>went on to</u> explain that the course <u>was</u> an opportunity to experience   A B C D
         A   **B**

   new challenges. Then he <u>said</u>, "By the end of your course, you
                         C

   <u>will have been learning</u> surprising things about yourself and your potential."
           D

VOCABULARY

 STRATEGY

> **DEALING WITH UNFAMILIAR VOCABULARY** You may encounter unknown words in the vocabulary section. Before answering, read through the question to determine the situation or topic. Then read each answer choice and decide which one best fits into the sentence. Do not be afraid to choose an unknown word, especially if you think the other choices are wrong.

Circle the letter of the word(s) which can best replace the boldface words in each sentence.

1. Translation can be difficult even for the most **seasoned**   A B Ⓒ D
   professionals.
   - **(A)** fluent   **(C)** experienced
   - **(B)** expert   **(D)** intellectual

2. Some **would-be** translators think that all you need is a good   A B C D
   command of the languages, but in fact, translation needs to be
   learned and practiced.
   - **(A)** future   **(C)** eager
   - **(B)** prospective   **(D)** younger

3. Simultaneous translation can be particularly **grueling**.   A B C D
   - **(A)** fun   **(C)** depressing
   - **(B)** difficult   **(D)** problematic

4. It can be helpful if a simultaneous translator is able to **foresee** the direction the speaker is going in.   A B C D
   (A) await   (C) prepare for
   (B) predict   (D) be interested in

5. Whenever **viable**, translators doing simultaneous translation should take frequent breaks.   A B C D
   (A) stressful   (C) necessary
   (B) fatigued   (D) possible

6. Translators doing written translation may find their decisions **daunting**.   A B C D
   (A) intimidating   (C) frustrating
   (B) inspiring   (D) exhausting

WRITING

> **ANSWERING ESSAY QUESTIONS** The writing sections of standardized tests are graded on a number of criteria. Two important criteria include essay organization and correct grammar. Be sure to create an outline so your essay will be organized. You should always have a clear introduction, a body, and a brief conclusion. Then, in writing your essay, play it safe. Stick to familiar grammar and vocabulary so you know there will be no mistakes. Use a combination of long and short sentences when possible.

1. Space exploration programs require an enormous amount of money which some believe would be better used for social problems. Supporters of space exploration believe that it will ultimately solve many of these problems and is worth the investment. What is your opinion of the amount of money spent on space exploration? Give reasons to support your opinion.

2. Your employees have been working hard for several months on a very stressful project. You want to reward them with a vacation. One idea is to send them on a challenging, team building adventure vacation. Alternatively, they could spend some time relaxing in the sun. Which vacation would you choose for your employees and why? Write an essay describing this vacation and what you hope your employees will get out of it. Give reasons to support your choice.

PRONUNCIATION SYMBOLS

Vowels

Symbol	Keyword
i	beat, feed
ɪ	bit, did
eɪ	date, paid
e	bet, bed
æ	bat, bad
ɑ	box, odd, father
ɔ	bought, dog
oʊ	boat, road
ʊ	book, good
u	boot, food, student
ʌ	but, mud, mother
ə	banana, among
ɚ	shirt, murder
aɪ	bite, cry, buy, eye
aʊ	about, how
ɔɪ	voice, boy
ɪr	beer
ɛr	bare
ɑr	bar
ɔr	door
ʊr	tour

Consonants

Symbol	Keyword
p	pack, happy
b	back, rubber
t	tie
d	die
k	came, key, quick
g	game, guest
tʃ	church, nature, watch
dʒ	judge, general, major
f	fan, photograph
ʋ	van
θ	thing, breath
ð	then, breathe
s	sip, city, psychology
z	zip, please, goes
ʃ	ship, machine, station, special, discussion
ʒ	measure, vision
h	hot, who
m	men, some
n	sun, know, pneumonia
ŋ	sung, ringing
w	wet, white
l	light, long
r	right, wrong
y	yes, use, music

GRAMMAR REFERENCE

Irregular Verbs

BASE FORM	SIMPLE PAST	PAST PARTICIPLE	BASE FORM	SIMPLE PAST	PAST PARTICIPLE
arise	arose	arisen	forgo	forwent	forgone
awake	awoke/awakened	awoke/awakened	freeze	frozen	frozen
be	was, were	been	get	got	gotten/got
bear	bore	borne	give	gave	given
beat	beat	beaten/beat	go	went	gone
become	became	become	grind	ground	ground
begin	began	begun	grow	grew	grown
bend	bent	bent	hang	hung	hung
bet	bet	bet	have	had	had
bite	bit	bitten	hear	heard	heard
bleed	bled	bled	hide	hid	hidden/hid
blow	blew	blown	hit	hit	hit
break	broke	broken	hold	held	held
bring	brought	brought	hurt	hurt	hurt
broadcast	broadcast/broadcasted	broadcast/broadcasted	keep	kept	kept
build	built	built	kneel	knelt/kneeled	knelt/kneeled
burn	burned/burnt	burned/burnt	knit	knit/knitted	knit/knitted
burst	burst	burst	know	knew	known
buy	bought	bought	lay	laid	laid
cast	cast	cast	lead	led	led
catch	caught	caught	leap	leaped/leapt	leaped/leapt
choose	chose	chosen	leave	left	left
cling	clung	clung	lend	lent	lent
come	came	come	let	let	let
cost	cost	cost	lie (down)	lay	lain
creep	crept	crept	light	lit/lighted	lit/lighted
cut	cut	cut	lose	lost	lost
deal	dealt	dealt	make	made	made
dig	dug	dug	mean	meant	meant
dive	dived/dove	dived	pay	paid	paid
do	did	done	prove	proved	proved/proven
draw	drew	drawn	put	put	put
dream	dreamed/dreamt	dreamed/dreamt	quit	quit/quitted	quit/quitted
drink	drank	drunk	read	read	read
drive	drove	driven	rid	rid/ridded	rid/ridded
eat	ate	eaten	ride	rode	ridden
fall	fell	fallen	ring	rang	rung
feed	fed	fed	rise	rose	risen
feel	felt	felt	run	ran	run
fight	fought	fought	saw	sawed	sawed/sawn
find	found	found	say	said	said
fit	fitted/fit	fitted/fit	see	saw	seen
flee	fled	fled	seek	sought	sought
fling	flung	flung	sell	sold	sold
fly	flew	flown	send	sent	sent
forbid	forbade/forbad	forbidden/forbid	set	set	set
forget	forgot	forgotten	sew	sewed	sewn/sewed
			shake	shook	shaken
			shave	shaved	shaved/shaven
			shear	sheared	sheared/shorn
			shine	shone	shone

164

Base Form	Simple Past	Past Participle	Base Form	Simple Past	Past Participle
shoot	shot	shot	strew	strewed	strewn
show	showed	shown	strike	struck	struck/striken
shrink	shrank/shrunk	shrunk/shrunken	swear	swore	sworn
			sweep	swept	swept
shut	shut	shut	swell	swelled	swelled/swollen
sing	sang	sung			
sink	sank	sunk	swim	swam	swum
sit	sat	sat	take	took	taken
slay	slew	slain	teach	taught	taught
sleep	slept	slept	tear	tore	torn
slide	slid	slid	tell	told	told
sneak	sneaked/snuck	sneaked/snuck	think	thought	thought
speak	spoke	spoken	throw	threw	thrown
speed	sped	sped	undergo	underwent	undergone
spend	spent	spent	understand	understood	understood
spill	spilled/spilt	spilled/spilt	upset	upset	upset
spin	spun	spun	wake	woke/waked	waked/woken
spit	spat/spit	spat/spit	wear	wore	worn
split	split	split	weave	wove/weaved	woven/weaved
spread	spread	spread	weep	wept	wept
spring	sprang/sprung	sprung	wet	wet/wetted	wet/wetted
stand	stood	stood	win	won	won
steal	stole	stolen	wind	wound	wound
stick	stuck	stuck	withdraw	withdrew	withdrawn
sting	stung	stung	wring	wrung	wrung
stink	stank	stunk	write	wrote	written

Common Stative Verbs

APPEARANCE	EMOTIONS	MENTAL STATES		PERCEPTION	OTHER
appear	abhor	agree	find	ache	cost
be	admire	amaze	guess	feel	include
concern	adore	amuse	hesitate	hear	lack
indicate	appreciate	annoy	hope	hurt	matter
look	care	assume	imagine	notice	owe
mean	desire	astonish	imply	observe	refuse
parallel	detest	believe	impress	perceive	suffice
represent	dislike	bore	infer	see	
resemble	doubt	care	know	sense	
seem	empathize	consider	mean	smart	
signify	envy	deem	mind	smell	
	fear	deny	presume	taste	
WANTS	hate	disagree	realize		
	hope	disbelieve	recollect	**POSSESSION**	
desire	like	entertain	remember		
need	love	estimate	revere	belong	
prefer	regret	expect	suit	contain	
want	respect	fancy	suppose	have	
wish	sympathize	favor	think	own	
	trust	feel	tire	pertain	
		figure	understand	possess	

Common Verbs Followed by the Gerund (Base Form of Verb + -ing)

abhor	confess	endure	imagine	postpone	resume
acknowledge	consider	enjoy	keep (=continue)	practice	risk
admit	defend	escape	keep on	prevent	shirk
advise	delay	evade	mention	put off	shun
allow	deny	explain	mind (=object to)	recall	suggest
anticipate	detest	fancy	miss	recollect	support
appreciate	discontinue	feel like	necessitate	recommend	tolerate
avoid	discuss	feign	omit	report	understand
be worth	dislike	finish	permit	resent	urge
can't help	dispute	forgive	picture	resist	warrant
celebrate	dread	give up (=stop)			

Common Verbs Followed by the Infinitive (To + Base Form of Verb)

agree	claim	fail	mean (=intend)	remain	tend
appear	come	get	need	request	threaten
arrange	consent	grow (up)	offer	resolve	turn out
ask	dare	guarantee	pay	say	venture
attempt	decide	hesitate	prepare	seek	volunteer
beg	demand	hope	pretend	seem	wait
can/can't afford	deserve	hurry	profess	shudder	want
can/can't wait	determine	incline	promise	strive	wish
care	elect	learn	prove	struggle	would like
chance	endeavor	manage	refuse	swear	yearn
choose	expect				

Common Verbs Followed by the Gerund or Infinitive

attempt	can't bear	continue	like	prefer	regret
begin	can't stand	hate	love	propose	start

Common Verbs Followed by the Gerund or the Infinitive with a Change in Meaning

forget	go on	quit	remember	stop	try

Common Verbs Followed by the Object + Infinitive

advise	choose*	expect*	hire	order	persuade	teach	want*
allow	convince	forbid	invite	pay*	remind	tell	warn
ask*	encourage	force	need*	permit	require	urge	would like
cause							

These verbs can also be followed by the infinitive without an object.

Common Inseparable Phrasal Verbs

advise against
apologize for
approve of
back out (of)
bear up
be familiar with
believe in
brush up (on)
carry on (with)
catch up (on)
choose between/
  among
come about
come across
come along
come apart
come around
come between
come by
come down with
come in
come into
come off
come out

come over
come through
come to
come up
come upon
come up with
complain about
count on
cut down on
deal with
do without
dream about/of
feel like
fill in for
follow up on
get about
get after
get ahead
get along (with)
get around
get away with
get back
get behind

get by (on)
get even (with)
get in
get into
get off
get on
get out of
get over
get rid of
get through
get through to
get through with
get to know
get up (=rise)
give up on
go back on
go in for
go through
hurry up to
insist on
keep up with
laugh at
let up

listen in on
listen to
live up to
look after
look at
look back on
look down on
look for
look forward to
look like
look out for
look up to
make up
  (=become
  friendly again)
make up for
miss out (on)
object to
part with
plan on
put up with
rely on
resort to

run across
run into
run out of
run through
stand up to
stick to
stoop to
succeed in
take after
take care of
talk about
think about
try out for
turn into
turn out for
turn up (=appear
  suddenly)
wait for
walk out on
watch out for
wonder about
work up to
write about

Common Separable Phrasal Verbs

bring about
bring along
bring around
bring in
bring on
bring over
bring through
bring up
call off
call up
clear up
cut off
cut up
do over
drop off

figure out
fill out
fill up
find out
get across
give away
give back
give up
hand out
have on
hold up
look over
look up
make up (=invent)

make up one's mind
  (=decide)
mix up
pay back
pick up
put across
put away
put off
put on
put out
run by/past
set aside
show off
stir up

take away
take back
take off (=remove)
take on
take over
take up
think over
try on
try out
turn down
turn off
turn on
turn up (=increase
  the volume)

WORD FORMATION

In English there are prefixes and suffixes that can be added to a word to change its meaning or its part of speech. Some common ones are shown here, with examples of how they are used to form words.

Verb Formation

The endings -**ize** and -**ify** can be added to many nouns and adjectives to form verbs, like this:

legal		legalize
modern	**-ize**	modernize
popular		popularize
scandal		scandalize

Elvis Presley helped to make rock 'n' roll more **popular**. *He* **popularized** *rock 'n' roll.*

beauty		beautify
pure	**-ify**	purify
simple		simplify
solid		solidify

These tablets make the water **pure**. *They* **purify** *the water.*

Adverb Formation

The ending -**ly** can be added to most adjectives to form adverbs, like this:

easy		easily
main	**-ly**	mainly
quick		quickly
stupid		stupidly

His behavior was **stupid**. *He behaved* **stupidly**.

Noun Formation

The endings -**er**, -**ment**, and -**ation** can be added to many verbs to form nouns, like this:

drive		driver
fasten	**-er**	fastener
open		opener
teach		teacher

John **drives** *a bus. He is a bus* **driver**.

amaze		amazement
develop	**-ment**	development
pay		payment
retire		retirement

Children **develop** *very quickly. Their* **development** *is very quick.*

admire		admiration
associate	**-ation**	association
examine		examination
organize		organization

The doctor **examined** *me carefully. She gave me a careful* **examination**.

The endings -**ty**, -**ity**, and -**ness** can be added to many adjectives to form nouns, like this:

cruel		cruelty
odd	**-ty**	oddity
pure	**-ity**	purity
stupid		stupidity

Don't be so **cruel**. *I hate* **cruelty**.

dark		darkness
deaf	**-ness**	deafness
happy		happiness
kind		kindness

It was very **dark**. *The* **darkness** *made it impossible to see.*

Adjective Formation

The endings -**y**, -**ic**, -**ical**, -**ful**, and -**less** can be added to many nouns to form adjectives, like this:

bush		bushy
dirt	**-y**	dirty
hair		hairy
smell		smelly

There was a bad **smell** *in the room. The room was very* **smelly**.

algebra		algebraic
atom	**-ic**	atomic
biology	**-ical**	biological
mythology		mythological

Her work involves research in **biology**. *She does* **biological** *research.*

| pain | **-ful** | painful |
| hope | | hopeful |

His broken leg caused him a lot of **pain**. *It was very* **painful**.

| pain | **-less** | painless |
| hope | | hopeless |

The operation didn't cause her any **pain**. *It was* **painless**.